The Science Discovery Book

Y0-BVQ-952

Distributed By
EDUCATIVE TOYS AND SUPPLIES
6416 Van Nuys Blvd.
Van Nuys, California 91401

The Science Discovery Book

ANTHONY D. FREDERICKS, Ed.D.
BRAD K. CRESSMAN, M.S. Ed.
ROBERT D. HASSLER, M. Ed.

Scott, Foresman and Company
Glenview, Illinois   London

ISBN 0-673-18344-0

1 2 3 4 5 6-MAL-91 90 89 88 87 86

CONTENTS

Life Science Activities

Physical Science Activities

Earth Science Activities

PREFACE

This book has been written by working science teachers who know the value of easy-to-follow science activities and projects. It can serve as a convenient and ready reference for the elementary teacher who wishes to stimulate and enhance an appreciation of scientific principles in students. A liberal sprinkling of these projects throughout the science curriculum can help develop successful thinkers and promote science as a worthwhile and enjoyable subject.

We believe that science instruction is more than just a series of classroom experiments. A well-rounded approach to science provides students with opportunities to use the processes of investigation and discovery. Meaningful, real-life activities focusing on a discovery approach to science help students gain a personal understanding of the world in which they live.

This book presents a variety of activities, experiments, and ideas designed to get children actively involved in the processes of science. These projects will stimulate students to:

1. Develop appropriate problem-solving techniques and critical thinking skills.
2. Use a variety of scientific processes.
3. Develop an understanding of basic concepts through interactions with materials and ideas.
4. Solve problems in divergent ways rather than look for absolute answers.
5. Use their world, environment, community, and home as a learning laboratory.

The forty-two projects in this book are organized around three areas essential to a well-rounded science education: life science, physical science, and earth science. The activities have been drawn from daily living experiences in each of these areas and focus on providing students with a better understanding of the scientific principles that underlie the world in which they live.

Although grade-level designations are provided, teachers will find that these projects can be used over a broad spectrum of pupils, talents, and grades. In fact, each project can be used with remedial, gifted, or "average" students, either in homogeneous or heterogeneous groups.

Most projects can be conducted in a variety of grouping patterns. Many of the activities provide students with the opportunity to work in small groups or pairs. While this may be a departure from the traditional whole-class presentation of science lessons, it does offer pupils the opportunity to share ideas, investigate options in a non-threatening environment, and discuss scientific processes. Adequate guidance and supervision is necessary, however, to help each group function properly and complete each project successfully.

We encourage you to read through each activity prior to introducing it to your class. This overview will provide you with the necessary background information as well as knowledge of needed materials, organizational steps, project design, and other special features. In addition, both the introduction and conclusion of each activity contain vital data important to student success and understanding.

We strongly suggest that you take sufficient time to discuss the purpose of each project prior to initiating any activity. It will be important for students to understand the relevance of specific activities to their everyday world as well as to their regular classroom work in science.

We also suggest that you solicit follow-up suggestions from your class for selected projects. If you encourage students to share their own viewpoints, modifications, or alternate procedures, you will be enhancing the learning experience and motivating students to apply their learning to a variety of other scientific encounters.

You are also urged to follow up each project with a class discussion. The process approach to science investigation demands an interactive dialogue between students and teacher as well as between student and student. Discussions offer students a chance to understand the relationship of these science activities to their own lives. Follow-up conversations also provide you with a means of evaluating the activities and your students' success in completing them.

One distinctive feature of these projects is the inclusion of two types of questions, closed and open ended. You have the option of selecting and sharing those questions you feel to be most relevant and those with which you are most comfortable. The open-ended questions allow children to use divergent thinking skills and to enjoy a feeling of success in coming up with their own answers. We encourage you to help students generate a multiplicity of responses to these queries and to discuss and evaluate the appropriateness of each response. The closed questions focus on convergent thinking skills. Although suggested answers are provided for your use, you may want to explore other options with your pupils as well. In fact, science skills will be enhanced when students realize that there may be more than one answer to a particular question. You are, of course, encouraged to develop any additional questions that will assist students in their scientific investigations.

Each project in this book can easily be integrated with the regular science text—an option that encourages fuller exploration of a concept or principle. By matching the objectives listed in the Contents with those presented in the classroom science text you can use both approaches to help students achieve a thorough understanding of specific concepts. You will also note a variety of both structured and unstructured activities in this book—a feature that increases instructional options and further enhances the regular science curriculum.

Whatever projects, grouping strategies, or instructional formats you choose, students' mastery of scientific principles is ensured through an interrelated process of concept formation and self-discovery. More important, the ultimate goal of these activities—to help students appreciate science as an enjoyable and worthwhile part of their lives—will be realized.

This book is intended to supplement and enhance the regular science text. By integrating these projects into the regular classroom curriculum you are ensured of a dynamic and interesting approach to scientific exploration. More important, your students will come to sense the value of science in their daily lives.

OBTAINING MATERIALS

The projects in this book have been designed to use a minimum of materials and to include items normally available in most schools or easily obtainable from students. To assist you in obtaining sufficient supplies from students, we have included a parent letter following the activity sections. We suggest that you photocopy this letter and the accompanying list of materials and pass them out to students. Ask each child to check on the list the items he or she can bring to school and take the list home. Encourage each pupil to contribute some materials to the classroom science center. As the items are brought in they can be assembled into the classroom science kits described in the next section.

Depending on the size of your class and on how rapidly materials are consumed, it may be necessary to send a follow-up letter to parents later in the year. This follow-up letter can be identical to the first one or can be a special one designed by you and your students to ask for specific items and materials.

CLASSROOM SCIENCE KITS

All of the necessary science materials can be collected and organized into three special kits. The lists on page xx indicate what should be included in each kit. We suggest that you copy these lists and store them with their respective kits. Each kit can be assembled in a cardboard box or plastic container. Students may wish to design a special area of the classroom to store the kits.

Each project in this book has been coded so that you will know which kits are necessary to carry out the project. The items in the kits will be used in a number of projects; therefore, you and your students may want to initiate a tracking system to ensure that adequate supplies are always on hand.

Some items will only be needed once for certain projects. You may want to send home a special note with some students in order to obtain these items—see the list of special materials on page xx.

RECORDING CHARTS

To help students record and keep track of the results of their projects, we have provided some recording sheets at the end of the book. These sheets can be used to develop line or bar graphs and to record information over a specified period of time. They can also be used as measuring tools for certain projects.

You can select the appropriate chart for a particular activity and make sufficient copies to pass out to students to record their data. Completed sheets can be kept in a folder or appropriate science notebook.

PROJECTS

Each of the projects in this book is considered to be complete in and of itself. The grade levels, suggested times, organization, materials, procedure, and follow-up activities are designed for ease of use and immediate classroom applicability. In addition, the introduction and conclusion for each project provide you with necessary background information. In sum, each project is designed to supplement any science text as well as stimulate a discovery approach to science.

THE PROCESSES OF SCIENCE

The study of science is dynamic. That is, children's daily contacts with the scientific world involve a constant interaction between the known and the unknown. New ideas are discovered and others are modified, strengthened, or rejected. What helps children develop a scientific outlook is the processes to which they are exposed in class. In other words, science should not be merely a study of finite answers but rather an application of processes that aid in discovering and learning about the world we live in. These universal processes apply to a wide range of learning opportunities for students—opportunities that help them think for themselves and apply more of what happens in the classroom to their own lives.

A process approach to science stimulates divergent thinking and provides a means for children to investigate their world based on what they know as well as on what they wish to discover. It is the teacher's responsibility to generate situations and opportunities that enable scientific investigations to occur both in and out of the classroom. Instead of creating a subject of facts and figures, teachers can help students explore science through a questioning process that stimulates thinking. The types of questions that teachers pose can encourage scientific discovery as a natural part of each lesson. In this way the study of science becomes open ended, encouraging creativity and divergence while at the same time respecting individual differences.

The following seven processes, which are used throughout this book, are designed to help you energize your science curriculum, making it relevant and practical for each of your students. We suggest that you devote the first week or two of the school year to an introduction of these processes. Plan some time for class discussions of each process as well as opportunities for a few introductory activities. Encourage students to suggest other appropriate activities for each process (these suggestions can be recorded in a class notebook). The enabling questions for each process provide possibilities for extended class discussions related to all of the projects in the book.

We strongly recommend that you include examples of each process within and throughout your science curriculum.

Observing

Observation involves all the primary senses: seeing, hearing, smelling, tasting, and touching. It is an immediate reaction to one's environment and is the source of knowledge that humans employ most. Children sometimes tend to overrely on their observational powers or do not use them in tandem with other investigative abilities. When students are provided with opportunities to evaluate and question their observational skills, they gain a sense of the importance of this process. Scientific skills are enhanced when pupils use observation in combination with other processes, such as predicting and experimenting.

INTRODUCTORY ACTIVITIES

1. Direct small groups of children to look out a window for one minute. Afterward, ask them to record everything they saw. Ask the groups to compare their lists.
2. Ask one child to come into the classroom and perform a series of four or five actions (sit on a chair, tie shoes, point with a pencil, and so on). Ask students to record the actions and compare their lists.
3. Have students listen to the radio for 30 to 60 seconds and afterward discuss all the sounds they heard.
4. Fill several paper bags with objects that vary in texture (wool, sandpaper, leather, and so on). Direct students to reach into the bag and describe the objects they feel.
5. Blindfold a student and ask him or her to taste bites of onion, celery, lettuce, and potato and describe the differences in taste. Repeat with other students.

1. How do your observations differ from (John's, Mary's)?
2. Can you offer an explanation for your observations?
3. Have you ever seen or heard anything similar to this?
4. Would your observations be identical if you were to do the same things again?

Classifying

Classifying is the process of assigning basic elements (words, thoughts, objects) to specific groups. All the items within a particular group share a basic relationship that may or may not be reflected in other groups. As new ideas are encountered they are added to previously formulated groups on the basis of similar elements. Classifying enhances scientific comprehension because it provides students with the opportunity to relate prior knowledge to new concepts.

INTRODUCTORY ACTIVITIES
1. Have students cut out magazine pictures that depict a particular class of animals (mammals, birds). These pictures may be collected into a class scrapbook.
2. Ask students to create mobiles or murals illustrating a particular class of words (nouns, adjectives).
3. Ask students to bring in different types of collections (rocks, butterflies, bottle caps, and so on) to share with the class.
4. Pupils may wish to start specimen boxes of various artifacts (animal bones, arrowheads, leaves, and so on).

ENABLING QUESTIONS
1. How are these items related?
2. How many different ways can you think of that these objects could be grouped?
3. Are there any similarities between these items and something else you may have seen at home or in your neighborhood?
4. Are there other categories in which some of these items could be placed?

Inferring

Inferring is the process of making educated guesses. Students often need to make conjectures and suppositions on the basis of a minimum of data. Inferring is of two types: deductive (going from the general to the specific) and inductive (going from the specific to the general). Making inferences requires students to have a sufficient background of personal experiences as well as opportunities and encouragement to draw tentative conclusions or explanations.

INTRODUCTORY ACTIVITIES
1. Have students look at a collection of photographs. Ask them to describe the emotions that various people show.
2. Show a foreign film to the class and ask students to speculate on what the characters are saying.
3. Read an exciting story to the class, but stop at a climatic point. Have students speculate as to what may happen next.
4. Show various street signs to the class and ask students to guess the meaning of each one.

ENABLING QUESTIONS
1. Why do you believe that?
2. Do you have a reason for saying that?
3. Can you think of any other possibilities?
4. Why didn't this come out the way we wanted it to?

Communicating

Communication is the means by which information is shared and disseminated. It involves not only interacting with others but organizing data so that it can be effectively passed on to others. Communicating can take many forms, including gestures, verbal and written responses, reading, listening, showing, and questioning. The effective communicator is one who is able to organize ideas in such a way that they will be immediately comprehended by others.

INTRODUCTORY ACTIVITIES

1. Direct a group of students to create their own form of sign language and to present a short demonstration of the language to the rest of the class. You may want to show them a book on sign language to give them some ideas.
2. Have some students study pictographs or hieroglyphics and make a report to the rest of the class.
3. Ask some pupils to choose several sentences from a specific chapter of the science book and to rewrite the sentences in random order. Give them to other students to write in the correct order.
4. Ask a student to describe an object in the classroom without using words. What methods of communication are most easily understood?

ENABLING QUESTIONS

1. Why is this easy (hard) to understand?
2. Can you show us another way to communicate this information?
3. What other information do we need to pass on to others about this project?
4. Why is it important for us to write (read, tell) this information?

Measuring

Scientists are constantly measuring. Measuring provides the scientist with the hard data necessary to confirm hypotheses and make predictions. It yields the first-hand information necessary for all other stages of the scientific investigation. Measuring includes gathering data on size, weight, quantity, and number. For obvious reasons it is important that this information be accurate and specific.

INTRODUCTORY ACTIVITIES

1. Direct groups of students to measure the height, width, and length of specific items in the room. Record this information on the chalkboard and question students on any discrepancies.
2. Bring in several boxes or bottles of commercial food items. Ask students to measure the contents of each to see whether they match the listed proportions and quantities on the package labels. Try to arrive at reasons for any differences.

3. Direct students to make charts of items in the room whose measurements change over time (kids, plants) and those that remain constant (desks, rugs). What characteristics are similar? What characteristics are different?
4. Ask students to look through various books (other than science books) and collect examples of words that deal with measurement. Have them organize these examples into a class notebook.

ENABLING QUESTIONS

1. Why do you think these two measurements differed?
2. Do you feel we need more data before we go on?
3. Do you think we should measure these again to see whether we are truly accurate?
4. If the size (weight) of this object were larger (smaller), how do you think it would affect our experiment?

Predicting

Scientific investigation is a constant process of making predictions. Predicting is the process of extrapolating information based on a minimum of data or on information already known. The scientist then tries to confirm or refute the prediction based on the gathering of new data. Predictions provide scientists with a roadmap by which they can conduct their experiments. They provide goals—albeit tentative ones—but at least something to aim for. The data-gathering process provides scientists with the evidence they need to verify their original predictions.

INTRODUCTORY ACTIVITIES

1. Ask students to make predictions about the next day's weather. List the predictions on the chalkboard. On the next day, share the weather report from the newspaper to determine the accuracy of the predictions.
2. Ask some students to predict the heights or weights of their classmates. Question them on how they could prove the accuracy of their predictions. Is there any information needed to assist in making such predictions?

3. Ask students to list the preliminary information they would need in order to make predictions concerning (a) the height of a building, (b) the length of a pencil, (c) the age of an adult, or (d) the time necessary to cook a food item.
4. Ask students to look through the newspaper to locate predictions other than the weather (horoscopes, sports scores, and so on). Lead a discussion on how these predictions are made.

ENABLING QUESTIONS

1. How did you arrive at your prediction?
2. What makes you feel that your prediction is accurate?
3. What evidence do you think we need to confirm or reject that prediction?
4. Do you have a reason for saying that?

Experimenting

By definition, a true scientist is one who is constantly experimenting. Through experimenting, ideas are proven or disproven and hypotheses are confirmed or denied. Experimentation involves the identification and control of variables in order to arrive at a cause-effect conclusion. Experimenting also involves manipulating data and assessing the results. Students need to understand that they conduct experiments every day, from watching ice cream melt to deciding on what clothes to wear outside. Scientific experimentation, however, involves a more formalized process, albeit one that also touches our everyday activities.

INTRODUCTORY ACTIVITIES

1. Direct groups of students to invent a "chalkboard washer" that improves the way the chalkboard looks in addition to saving time and labor.
2. Provide students with several thermometers, glass jars, magnifying glasses, and lights. Challenge them to create a situation that raises the temperature of the air in each glass. Ask them to explain their procedures.
3. Ask students to create a musical scale using soda bottles or jars and measured quantities of water.
4. Have a group of students design an experiment for younger pupils that demonstrates the processes of condensation and evaporation.

ENABLING QUESTIONS

1. What else could we have done to arrive at this conclusion?
2. Is there another experiment we might do to arrive at the same conclusion?
3. Do we need any more evidence before we can say that?
4. Why do you think we did this experiment?

SCIENTIFIC INQUIRY TECHNIQUE

The Scientific Inquiry Technique is a method that stimulates active student involvement with text materials. It is a procedure teachers can use to tie the regular curriculum and text with a student-initiated questioning process to ultimately enhance scientific concept formation. Students are provided with opportunities to initiate their own questions, thus laying the foundations for text comprehension. This strategy helps students define the relationships between their own experiences and the ideas presented within a chapter or unit in their text.

The Scientific Inquiry Technique can be used in a variety of instructional formats, including whole-class and large- or small-group arrangements. Most important, it can become a regular feature of students' discoveries in science.

This technique involves the following steps:

1. A chapter or unit in the science text is chosen for the class to discuss.
2. The title of the chapter is recorded on the chalkboard, and discussion is initiated concerning the questions that students may have about the title or subject matter. All questions are recorded.
   a. "What questions come to mind when you see this title?" *(INFERRING)*
   b. "What kinds of questions would you like to ask the author of this book?" *(OBSERVING, CLASSIFYING)*

   Unit titles can also be recorded, along with related student questions.
3. The class discusses the topic, making guesses about the content of the chapter. The class then decides on the questions they feel to be most appropriate for exploration.
   a. "Are there any questions you would like to ask that we have used for other chapters?" *(CLASSIFYING)*
   b. "What do you think would be an important question to put on a test about this chapter?" *(COMMUNICATING)*
4. The class examines any illustrations in the chapter and poses questions about them.
   a. "What questions would you like to ask the artist of this drawing?" *(OBSERVING)*
   b. "Can you think of some questions younger (older) students would ask about these illustrations?" *(INFERRING)*

   The same procedure can be used for the unit sections as well.
5. The class participates in reading the chapter, looking for answers to their posed questions.

This reading may be oral or silent, depending on the dynamics of the group. As the selection is read, students are encouraged to develop additional questions that can also be recorded on the chalkboard. As answers to questions are found, the class talks about them and attempts to resolve any discrepancies between answers.

6. Upon completion of the chapter, the class discusses the recorded questions and the answers provided in the passage. The group attempts to reach a commonality of agreement on the appropriate answers. Questions that were not answered are also discussed, with students suggesting possible answers or reasons why the information was not located. Students may wish to refer back to the chapter to answer any questions.
7. The group may engage in a follow-up discussion using some of the following ideas:
   a. "What additional information do you feel should have been included in this chapter? What information could have been left out?"
   b. "Is there a better title for this chapter? If so, what would you suggest?"
   c. "How would this chapter be different if . . . ?"
   d. "What would happen if . . . ?"
   e. "What have you done or seen that may be similar to the ideas presented in this section?"

The Scientific Inquiry Technique stimulates students to assume a more active role in discovering the processes of science. Based on a model of reading comprehension, it guides students toward higher-level thinking skills and fosters the development of divergent reasoning. As students take responsibility for initiating and answering their own questions, they begin to appreciate the dynamic nature of scientific exploration. Facilitating this process can be an important aspect of your classroom science curriculum.

Classroom Kits

KIT 1—ART SUPPLIES

- [ ] food coloring
- [ ] paint
- [ ] paper clips
- [ ] clay
- [ ] aluminum foil
- [ ] waxed paper
- [ ] sponges
- [ ] crayons
- [ ] masking tape
- [ ] scissors
- [ ] construction paper
- [ ] colored cellophane
- [ ] cotton
- [ ] graph paper
- [ ] oaktag
- [ ] gum erasers
- [ ] drawing paper
- [ ] string
- [ ] cardboard
- [ ] newspaper
- [ ] plastic bags
- [ ] cellophane tape
- [ ] glue
- [ ] wire screening
- [ ] paper fasteners
- [ ] hole puncher
- [ ] insulated wire
- [ ] index cards
- [ ] colored pencils
- [ ] tablet paper
- [ ] styrofoam cups
- [ ] chalk
- [ ] plastic wrap—one roll
- [ ] notebook paper

KIT 2—MEASURING SUPPLIES

- [ ] rulers
- [ ] measuring cups
- [ ] spoons
- [ ] knives
- [ ] jars
- [ ] paper cups
- [ ] magnifying glasses
- [ ] stopwatch
- [ ] thermometers
- [ ] test tubes
- [ ] baby food jars
- [ ] plastic milk cartons
- [ ] coat hangers
- [ ] plastic glasses
- [ ] pill or film containers
- [ ] yogurt containers with lids
- [ ] meter sticks
- [ ] bobby pins
- [ ] balance
- [ ] coffee cans
- [ ] sprinkling can
- [ ] medicine dropper
- [ ] narrow flask
- [ ] spring scale
- [ ] microscope
- [ ] metric cups
- [ ] teaspoons

KIT 3—MISCELLANEOUS

- [ ] paper towels
- [ ] toothpicks
- [ ] seeds
- [ ] copper wire
- [ ] candles
- [ ] magnets
- [ ] steel pins
- [ ] corks
- [ ] sand
- [ ] rubber tubing
- [ ] baking soda
- [ ] stones
- [ ] paper bags
- [ ] shallow cake dish
- [ ] marbles
- [ ] jar lids
- [ ] pepper
- [ ] batteries
- [ ] stockings
- [ ] petroleum jelly
- [ ] shoe boxes
- [ ] golf balls
- [ ] playground balls
- [ ] peat moss
- [ ] buttons
- [ ] paper napkins
- [ ] popsicle sticks
- [ ] pencils
- [ ] salt
- [ ] filter paper
- [ ] lima bean seeds
- [ ] flashlights
- [ ] grass seed
- [ ] facial tissue
- [ ] sugar
- [ ] balloons
- [ ] soil
- [ ] wool
- [ ] straws
- [ ] pennies
- [ ] matches
- [ ] cigar box
- [ ] metal washers
- [ ] golf tees
- [ ] clay
- [ ] combs
- [ ] radish seeds
- [ ] birdseed
- [ ] baseballs
- [ ] sugar cubes
- [ ] pebbles
- [ ] clay soil
- [ ] bottle caps
- [ ] hard candy

SPECIAL MATERIALS

- [ ] carrots
- [ ] lima beans
- [ ] five-gallon aquarium or large bucket
- [ ] plastic
- [ ] fur
- [ ] colored sponges
- [ ] two light projectors
- [ ] flat piece of cardboard
- [ ] cans of 7-Up
- [ ] bleach
- [ ] earthworms
- [ ] pine cones
- [ ] peanut butter
- [ ] crackers
- [ ] dry soup mix
- [ ] egg
- [ ] mealworms
- [ ] silicon glue
- [ ] alcohol
- [ ] bran, oats, cornflakes
- [ ] celery
- [ ] emery cloth
- [ ] steel and lead foil
- [ ] brass foil
- [ ] aspirin
- [ ] nickels
- [ ] Karo syrup
- [ ] noodles
- [ ] rice
- [ ] iced tea mix
- [ ] flour
- [ ] ice cubes
- [ ] apples
- [ ] bread
- [ ] cranberry juice

Life Science

A C T I V I T I E S

Life. It's all around us. From Rover barking in the backyard to the plants in the living room to the tiny speck of mold on the kitchen counter, we are surrounded by life. Understanding how plants and animals grow and develop as well as how they interact with each other is an important part of science. In many ways, life is the area of the scientific world with which students are most familiar and is truly a field ripe for exploration. As students gain an awareness of the life forms around them, they also develop an appreciation for their own place in the gigantic ecosystem that we all participate in every day.

This section introduces your students to several of the life sciences. Some of the projects offer a look into botany: how plants survive, the environments they live in, and how they reproduce. Other projects provide insights into ecology, the relationship between living things and their environment by having students conduct population studies and examine camouflage techniques, for example. Still other activities explore physiology—how the body operates—and zoology, from microscopic life to worms to birds.

The study of life in all its forms is one of the basics of science. As students learn about patterns of growth, ecological relationships, and environmental habitats, they gain an appreciation for the majesty of the world around them. This knowledge can then be used in efforts to preserve the living world for successive generations.

HEY, WHAT'S INSIDE? (SEEDS, PART I)

KITS NEEDED: **Kit 1, 2, 3**   GRADE LEVEL: **4–5**

SUGGESTED TIME: Two 50-minute periods

Introduction

Students will learn first-hand that within each seed is a tiny plant. They will discover how this tiny plant is able to emerge from the seed and will learn what conditions favor or hamper seed germination. These concepts are developed in this project and the next two ("Seeds," parts II and III). These three activities may be carried out independently of one another or in succession. This initial project provides students with an opportunity to examine the outside and inside of a seed.

Organization and Materials

Students can work individually or in pairs.

Per Group: One lima bean, a magnifying glass, a collection of various kinds of seeds (flower, apple, orange, and so on), paper, container of water.

Procedure

1. Lead a discussion to determine what students know about seeds. Distribute various kinds of seeds to the class to inspect during the discussion.

"What is a seed?"
"Where do seeds come from?"
"Are all seeds the same?"
"How are they alike? How are they different?"
"What do we use seeds for?"
"Where do new plants come from?" "How does this happen?"

(Acknowledge all answers for now, but refrain from confirming or disputing any hypotheses.)
(COMMUNICATING, INFERRING, OBSERVING)

2. Distribute a lima bean, a sheet of paper, and a magnifying glass to each student or group. Have the students examine the seed. Tell them to look closely at the seed and then draw what they see on their paper. *(OBSERVING, COMMUNICATING)*

3. Soak the seeds in water overnight.

4. The next day, distribute the seeds to the students and have them examine the seeds again, carefully and closely. Instruct them to look for any changes. Discuss the changes they observe. Have the students sketch how the seed appears to them now. *(OBSERVING, COMMUNICATING)*

5. Have the students gently open the seed along its natural opening (a demonstration may be necessary). Stress how gently this must be done. *(EXPERIMENTING)*

6. Have the students observe what they see inside the seed. (They should be able to find a tiny plant.) *(OBSERVING)*

7. Discuss the findings.
"What did you find?"
"What do you think happens to this tiny plant when a seed is planted?" (It develops into a plant.)
"What do you think all the material inside the seed is needed for?" (Food.)
"Why is the outside of the seed so hard?" (Protection.)
(OBSERVING, COMMUNICATING, INFERRING)

8. Have the students make sketches of the inside of their seed. *(COMMUNICATING)*

Conclusion

Within each seed, a tiny plant is found. This tiny plant, called the embryo, is the beginning of a new plant. The other materials inside the seed provide the nutrients for the new plant to begin growing, developing, and thriving until it can take in sustenance on its own.

Follow-up Activities

1. See "Seeds" parts II and III (Life Science Activities 2 and 3).
2. Investigate other seeds in the same manner.
3. Have students try to open a seed without soaking it in water (this leads to "Seeds," Part II).

THE SOGGY SEED (SEEDS, PART II)

KITS NEEDED: **Kit 1, 2, 3** GRADE LEVEL: **4—6**

SUGGESTED TIME: Two 50-minute periods

Introduction

By performing an experiment with lima beans, students learn that water enters seeds through a tiny opening called the microphyle. This opening is located in the seam, or scar, of the seed and enables the seed to take up water so that it can germinate.

Organization and Materials

Divide students into groups of two or three each.

Per Group: Six lima beans (make sure seed coats are free of any cracks), a container of water, a candle, matches, water-resistant glue, a magnifying glass.

Procedure

1. Review the concepts developed in "Seeds," Part I.

"What is inside a seed?" (Tiny plant, embryo.)

"When seeds are planted and the plants begin to grow, where do these plants come from?" (Inside the seed.)

"How were we able to look inside a seed to see the tiny plant called the embryo?"
(COMMUNICATING, INFERRING)

2. Distribute six seeds to each group.

3. Have the students examine their seed with and without a magnifying glass.

"How could water get inside the seed to soften it?" (Accept all answers.)

"Can you find a spot where the water could get into the seed?"   *(OBSERVING, INFERRING)*

4. "How could we determine whether this spot allows water to enter the seed?" (Have students formulate a test to determine whether their hypothesis is correct. Students should come to the realization that if the hole is clogged, the seed will have difficulty absorbing water.)

"How could we clog up this hole?" (Allow students to offer suggestions.)
(INFERRING, COMMUNICATING, PREDICTING)

5. Have students place a drop of candle wax (or any other waterproof sealant) on the tiny spot of three of their six seeds, and tell them to mark these seeds with a water-resistant pen.

6. After the drops dry, have students place all the seeds in a container of water to soak overnight.

7. The next day, examine the seeds and discuss the findings.

"How have the seeds changed?"

"Did all the seeds change?"

"Which seeds did change and which did not change?" (The seeds that were waterproofed will not have expanded and cracked as much as those not waterproofed.)

"What do your results tell you about seeds?" (The tiny hole in the seed allows water to enter.)

"Why is it important for water to enter a seed?" (To soften it and allow the tiny plant to emerge.)
(OBSERVING, COMMUNICATING, INFERRING)

Conclusion

The three seeds whose holes were clogged did not change. The three plain seeds, without the clogged holes, swelled up and were easy to take apart. Water enters the seed through the microphyle and softens it so that the embryo can break through the covering and begin to grow.

Follow-up Activities

1. Have students try the same experiment using other types of vegetable seeds.

2. Have students soak two seeds in water (one clogged, one unclogged) and plant them along with two unsoaked seeds (one clogged, one unclogged). Ask pupils to predict which seeds will germinate. Growth patterns can be charted and recorded.

POP GOES
THE PLANT
(SEEDS, PART III)

KITS NEEDED: **Kit 1, 2**　　**GRADE LEVEL:** **4−6**

SUGGESTED TIME: One 50-minute period, plus 5−10 minutes per day of observation time

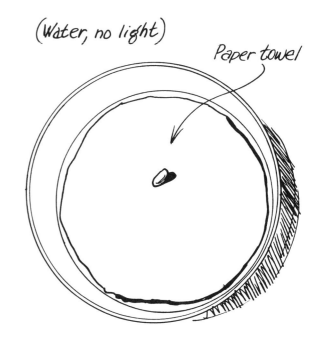

(Water, no light)

Paper towel

Introduction

Several environmental conditions contribute to the ability of seeds to germinate. How rapidly a seed germinates and how many seeds of a given species will germinate during a given time period are determined by such factors as temperature, moisture, and oxygen. In this activity students attempt to germinate seeds to learn about conditions that favor and speed germination.

Organization and Materials

This activity is best suited for groups of three to four students.

Per Group: Six radish seeds (or substitute), six yogurt or milk containers, paper towels (cut to fit the containers), water, melted wax or silicon glue. (*Optional:* Six plastic bags to place the containers in for speeding germination.)

Procedure

1. Review the concepts presented in "Seeds," parts I and II.

"What did we find out about seeds?" (They contain tiny plants, water is needed to soften the seed so the plant can emerge, water enters the seed through a tiny hole in the seed coat, and the seed contains nutrients for the tiny plant.)

"Where does a new plant come from when a seed is planted?"

"How does the new plant get out of the seed?"

"What does the seed need to have in order for the new plant to be able to grow?"
(COMMUNICATING, INFERRING)

2. Have the students set up the milk or yogurt containers as follows: (a) Moisten a piece of paper towel and place it in each container. (b) Put a seed in each container. (c) Vary conditions for the containers as follows:

Container 1—paper towel, water, no light, room temperature.

Container 2—paper towel, water, light, room temperature.

Container 3—paper towel, no water, light, room temperature.

Container 4—no paper towel (seed floating in water), light, room temperature.

Container 5—paper towel, water, no light, kept in refrigerator or freezer.

Container 6—paper towel, no water, no light, room temperature, seed covered with wax.
(EXPERIMENTING)

3. Have students record the germination dates on the containers as they occur.

4. Discuss the results.

"Which seeds germinated?"

"Is light (water, temperature, growing medium) needed for a seed to germinate?" (Water and favorable temperature are necessary.)

"What conditions hamper the germination of seeds?" (Lack of moisture, extreme temperatures, and wax covering.)
(COMMUNICATING, INFERRING, CLASSIFYING)

Conclusion

Seeds need favorable temperature, adequate moisture, and oxygen to germinate. Light is not needed for germination.

Follow-up Activities

1. Have students perform the same experiment with a variety of other seeds.

2. Have students alter the environmental conditions (heat, light, nutrients) for selected seeds and chart the germination patterns over an extended period of time.

ROOTS AND ROUTES

KITS
NEEDED: **Kit 2, 3**   GRADE
LEVEL: **4–6**

SUGGESTED
TIME: One 50-minute period, plus follow-up observations

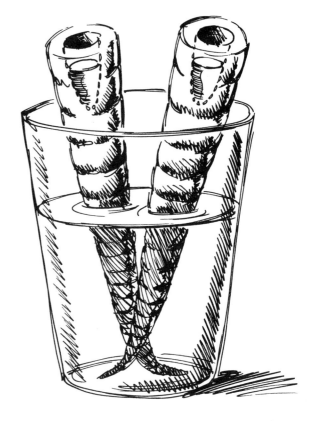

Introduction

For plants and animals to grow, they must take in nutrients. We know how that is done by animals, but what about plants—how do they obtain nutrients? In this activity students will learn that the root system collects and transports the water and nutrients the plant needs. A familiar root, the carrot, helps demonstrate this process.

Organization and Materials

This lesson is intended for small-group demonstrations. Divide the class into groups of no more than four students each.

Per Group: A jar or glass, two carrots, water, sugar water (4 tablespoons of sugar to 1 quart of water), knife, paper towels.

Note: Keep carrots refrigerated until ready for use.

Procedure

1. Cut off the tops of two carrots and hollow out the centers to a depth of one inch.

2. Have each group fill a glass with tap water to within two inches of the top.

"Why don't we fill the glass all the way to the top?" (When the carrots are put into the glass, the water will flow over the top.)   *(INFERRING)*

3. Have the groups set two carrots in each glass (cut portion on top).

"What do you observe about the water level in the glass when the carrots are put in?" (The water level rises.)   *(OBSERVING)*

4. Have students fill the hollow part of one carrot with tap water and the hollow part of the other carrot with sugar water (each should be filled halfway to the top).

"Is it important to put the same amount of liquid in each carrot?" "Why?" (All the variables must be controlled.)

(INFERRING, EXPERIMENTING)

5. Place each glass away from the sun until the following day.

"Why is it better to place the glass away from the sun?"   *(INFERRING)*

"Do you think any other factors in the room will affect the outcome of the experiment?"

(INFERRING)

6. The next day observe the carrots and note any changes.

"How can you account for the difference in the water levels inside the two carrots?" (Refer to the Conclusion.)

"Why would this be important to the survival of carrots or any other plants?"

(OBSERVING, INFERRING)

7. Have the students repeat this experiment with other plants (turnips, beets, celery, potatoes, corn stalks, and so on).

"What differences do you note between plants normally grown underground and those grown above ground?"

"What differences do you note between plants with a high sugar content (beets, corn) and those with a low sugar content (celery)?" *(OBSERVING)*

Conclusion

The students should see that the carrot containing sugar water has more water in its hollow the day after the project began. This is because the natural sugars found in plants are attracted by the sugar water. These sugars are acting as the nutrients of the plant.

Follow-up Activities

1. Have the students repeat the experiment using other substances in place of sugar (salt, juice, gelatin) to determine whether these substances could be used as nutrients for plants.

2. Fill a glass with water half way. Invert the carrot in a clear glass, making sure no water enters the hollow. Have students predict how the hollow will look when the carrot is immersed in various liquids.

LIFE **5** SCIENCE

GREEN HIGHWAYS

KITS NEEDED: **Kit 1**   GRADE LEVEL: **4–6**

SUGGESTED TIME: One 50-minute period, plus periodic observations

Introduction

The stem of a plant is responsible for transporting water and nutrients to the rest of the plant. Conducting tubes in the stem carry water upward to the branches, leaves, and flowers.

Organization and Materials

Divide the class into groups of three or four.

Per Group: One stalk of celery, two glasses of water, red food coloring, knife.

Note: The celery stalks can be precut, except for one to be used as a demonstration. If possible, complete this experiment early in the day.

Procedure

1. Have each group fill one glass with clear water and the other with water containing four drops of red food coloring.

"Does it matter if the glasses are equally full?" (Yes.)

"Why?" (It is important to control all variables.) *(INFERRING)*

2. Have students cut one inch off the bottom of each celery stalk.

"Why is it important to cut the bottom off the celery?" (By cutting the bottom off the plant, you remove the bacteria that would block the entry of water.) *(INFERRING)*

3. Ask students to cut each stalk up the middle about halfway, then put one of the celery ends in the glass containing clear water and the other end in the glass containing red food coloring.

4. Have students observe the celery every hour and note all changes.

"Why is it important to record this information accurately?" (Careful record keeping is important in science.) *(OBSERVING)*

"Is the change in the celery sudden or gradual?" "Why?" *(INFERRING)*

5. Have students record results the next day by cutting both bottom sides every inch and noting the location of the red water.

"What causes the celery to get red?" (The flow of red water throughout the plant.) *(INFERRING)*

FEED ME, I'M YOURS

KITS NEEDED: **Kit 2**   GRADE LEVEL: **4—5**

SUGGESTED TIME: One 50-minute period, plus four weeks of brief daily observations

Introduction

Fresh-cut flowers brighten the day, no matter what the occasion. Unfortunately, the time of enjoyment is short-lived, as most flowers quickly begin to turn brown and wither. If we give them the proper nourishment, however, we can lengthen the time of enjoyment considerably.

Organization and Materials

Because of the ongoing nature of this project, it is best to divide the class into three groups, each following the same steps.

Per Group: Several flowers (carnations are ideal), one can of lemon-lime soda, two aspirin, one can of water, two teaspoons of sugar, four quart jars, liquid bleach.

Procedure

1. With the class, list the basic needs of plants. Discuss how these needs might change when the plant is cut, thus leaving it without a root system.

"What will happen if we cut a flower?"
(PREDICTING)

2. Instruct the groups to cut off the bottom of each flower at the base of the stem. (*Hint:* The stem's surface area is increased if it is cut off at an angle.)

"Why would it be beneficial to cut the stem on an angle?" (Refer to hint.)   *(INFERRING)*

3. Have students mix the following solutions separately and add them to the jars: Jar A—plain water: Jar B—dissolved aspirin in water: Jar C—dissolved sugar in water: Jar D—one-half can of lemon-lime soda, one-half can of water, seven drops of liquid bleach (the bleach provides a deterrent to bacteria buildup at the base of the stem, thus allowing the soda solution to travel up the stem).

"What reasons can you offer for trying the different types of solutions?" (To see whether plants respond differently to various solutions; to identify those components necessary for plant survival.)   *(INFERRING)*

Conclusion

Nutrients dissolved in water travel from the ground up the stems of a plant in conducting tubes. In this way all parts of the plant get the water and nourishment they need to grow and develop.

Follow-up Activities

1. Have students repeat the experiment using fresh-cut flowers (carnations work well).
2. Have students cut a large celery stalk into four parts, putting each part into a different color of water.
3. Have students experiment with other edible plants by placing them in colored water and recording the results.

4. Tell students to put two flowers into each of the four jars.

"Which group of flowers will last the longest?" "Why?" *(PREDICTING, INFERRING)*

5. Have the students draw pictures of the flowers as they appear on this date.

6. Direct students to record daily observations or notes on a chart for four weeks, noting any changes in the appearance of the flowers.

Conclusion

Plants need water and food to survive. The types of nutrients a plant gets from its environment will determine, in large measure, how well it will endure and thrive. In this activity the sugar acts as the necessary food for the flower. Plants prosper because they have adapted to those environmental conditions that facilitate their survival.

Follow-up Activities

1. Have students repeat the activity changing either the type of flower or the solutions.

2. Have students attempt to reproduce the soda-bleach solution in dry form by getting the ingredients off the labels.

FOLLOW THAT LIGHT

KITS NEEDED: **Kit 1, 3**   GRADE LEVEL: **4–5**

SUGGESTED TIME: One 50-minute period, plus several periodic observations

Introduction

Plants need sunlight to survive. Through a process within plants known as phototropism, they continually seek a light source. The normal vertical growth pattern of plants will change to satisfy this need.

Organization and Materials

This activity is best suited for groups of three or four students.

Per Group: Two shoe boxes, one bean plant, scissors.

Procedure

1. Have students label their shoe boxes Box A and Box B. Tell them to cut off the end of Box A and cut a section the same size in the middle of a long side of Box B. The cut ends should be placed together to form a T (see illustration).

2. Instruct students to cut a 2-inch hole at one end of Box B.

3. Have students place the bean plant in Box A at the end farthest from Box B, then place both lids on the boxes (the lids may need to be cut to size) and tape them.

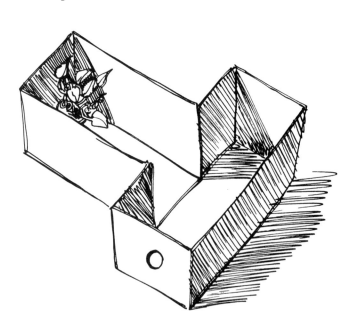

4. Have students position the boxes so that the hole is facing a source of light.

"How will the bean plant react to this situation?" (The plant will grow toward the light.) *(INFERRING)*

5. Every two days, have students carefully remove the lids to water the plant and record any growth that has taken place. Have them draw and measure the progress of the plant.

"Why is the plant reacting in this manner?" (The plant is seeking a light source.) *(COMMUNICATING, INFERRING)*

6. Have students continue to observe and record the growth rate and direction of growth for a three-week period.

"Is the direction of growth with this plant any different than the growth observed in other normally growing plants?" "Why?" (Yes. Most plants, under normal growing conditions, will grow in a vertical direction.)

"What would happen if we put a hole in both ends of Box B?" (The plant would grow toward the stronger light source.) *(INFERRING)*

Conclusion
Plants seek out light. For plants to find light, they must make adjustments in their normal growth pattern.

Follow-up Activities
1. Have students repeat the activity altering either the intensity or color of the light. Compare the results.

2. Have students construct several mazes in which plants must seek a light source.

PLANTS BREATHE, TOO

KITS NEEDED: **Kit 1, 2, 3**   GRADE LEVEL: **4—6**

SUGGESTED TIME: One 50-minute period, followed by two weeks of observations

Introduction
The needs of a green plant are most easily met when that plant is situated in the proper environment. These needs include water, sunlight, heat, and air. When any of these needs are not met, proper growth of the plant is no longer possible.

Organization and Materials
This activity is best suited for groups of four or five students.

Per Group: Three bean plants, petroleum jelly, drawing paper, ruler.

Procedure
1. Have students position bean plants so that each will receive equal amounts of sunlight and water. The plants should be labeled A, B, and C.

2. Have students draw a picture of each plant and measure and record the height of each. *(OBSERVING, MEASURING)*

3. Direct students to rub petroleum jelly on the top side of all the leaves of Plant A and on the underside of the leaves of Plant B.

"Do you think that the petroleum jelly will cause a change in the leaves of these plants?"

"If there is a change in the plants, can you predict what that change will be?" *(INFERRING, PREDICTING)*

4. Allow the third plant to remain as it is—to act as a control.

"Why do you think a 'control' is an important part of any experiment?" (It is necessary to have a normal plant with which to compare the others.) *(COMMUNICATING, INFERRING)*

5. Every other day, have students record the height of each plant and draw pictures showing any changes that have taken place.

"Can you explain why the growth rates in the plants are different?"

"What conclusion can be drawn from observing Plants A and B?" (Refer to the Conclusion.) *(INFERRING, OBSERVING, COMMUNICATING, MEASURING)*

Conclusion

Air is a necessary component for the chemical reaction called photosynthesis. The air enters the plant through the underside of the leaves. This explains why Plant B reacted as it did.

Follow-up Activities

1. Have students repeat this activity but this time put petroleum jelly on both the upper and lower sides of only certain leaves of a plant.

2. Have students experiment with other plants to see whether air is taken in by any other means. A plastic bag could be taped around the base of one plant, covering the soil and the container, uncovering only to water. Petroleum jelly could be rubbed onto the stem of another plant. Have students compare the results.

ADOPT A TREE

KITS NEEDED: **Kit 1, 2**   GRADE LEVEL: **4—6**

SUGGESTED TIME: Throughout the entire school year

Introduction

Trees, by the very nature of their size and abundance, are probably the most familiar of plants. Not only are they enjoyed for their beauty, but they also provide us with oxygen, food, and shelter. It is through a better understanding of trees that we can guarantee their preservation.

Organization and Materials

This is a whole class activity.

Per Class: String, ruler, crayons, drawing paper, writing paper.

Note: this activity is intended to be pursued throughout the school year. Steps 2 through 5 should be repeated during each of the four seasons (depending on your area of the country). An ongoing, cumulative display of the project will help motivate the students.

Procedure

1. Locate a deciduous tree close to your school. (*Hint:* Deciduous trees are those that shed their leaves annually.)

2. Have students draw a picture of the tree's general appearance and record any peculiarities.

"What distinguishing characteristics do you notice?"

"Why would the tree have these characteristics?"

"What changes have taken place since the tree was last observed?" *(OBSERVING, INFERRING)*

3. Measure three feet up the tree from the ground and wrap the piece of string around the tree at that point. Measure the string to determine the circumference of the trunk.

"Do you believe the circumference of the tree changes with the seasons?"

"Why?"

"Why did we put the string exactly three feet from the bottom?" (The string serves as a point of reference for future observations.)
(INFERRING, MEASURING)

4. Have students take several leaves back to the classroom. Direct them to place a leaf, vein side up, on a desk. Have them lay a piece of paper on top of the leaf and crayon the paper until the outline of the leaf appears.

"What similarities or differences can you see in the vein patterns of the various leaves?" (Record these observations on the chalkboard.)
(OBSERVING)

5. Direct students to hold a piece of paper against the bark of the tree. With a crayon, have them rub the paper until the bark pattern appears.

6. Repeat steps 2 through 5 at periodic intervals throughout the year. Compare and discuss the results. *(OBSERVING, COMMUNICATING)*

7. *Optional:* Take photographs of the tree at various times during the year. Mount them in a class scrapbook along with leaf samples and bark rubbings obtained at the same times the photos were taken.

Conclusion

Each season brings about changes in plant life. These changes are a necessary function of the plant for it to adjust to the environment.

Follow-up Activities

1. Using the fallen seeds from your adopted tree, have the class attempt to grow more trees. The seeds can be planted during an Arbor Day ceremony.

2. Have students write and distribute a brochure explaining the changes a tree goes through and describing how to properly care for it. Check with your county agricultural agent or local forestry department to obtain some sample leaflets or brochures.

LIFE **10** SCIENCE

THIS CAN'T BE A PLANT

KITS NEEDED: **Kit 1, 2**   GRADE LEVEL: **4–6**

SUGGESTED TIME: One 50-minute period, plus 10–15 minutes per day thereafter for 5–8 days

Introduction
Quite often we think of plants as green organisms with stems and leaves. But a wide variety of plants do not have these characteristics. In this activity students grow some simple nongreen plants and study the conditions affecting plant growth.

Organization and Materials
Students should be divided into groups of three or four each.

Per Group: One moldy piece of apple or orange, several plastic sandwich bags, baby food jars and lids (or plastic cups with covers), specimens to be tested (be sure to include one food specimen with moisture, such as bread, and one nonfood specimen without moisture, such as a stone), water, an eyedropper (or plastic straw), graph paper or a ruler to measure growth, colored pencils, magnifying glass.

Note: By enclosing the specimens in plastic sandwich bags, students can observe and measure specimen growth without handling the mold. Graph paper can be used to measure growth by placing the appropriate-size paper over the growth and counting squares.

Procedure
1. Have the students discuss and describe the types of plants with which they are most familiar (students will most likely list various green plants).

"This activity will introduce you to some plants that are very different from the ones you know best." *(COMMUNICATING)*

2. Show the class the moldy fruit and have the students observe and discuss the mold's characteristics. *(OBSERVING, COMMUNICATING)*

3. "Have you ever seen this type of plant before?" "Where?" (Accept various answers.)

"What characteristics make it different from other plants?" (Not leafy or green.)

"What characteristics make it similar to other plants?" (It is living and has "roots.") *(COMMUNICATING)*

4. "Why does it grow on this substance?" (Food is available.)

"Are there similar substances it might grow on?" (Accept all hypotheses.)

"What characteristics does this substance have that may be conducive to growth?" (Moisture, food source.)   *(INFERRING, COMMUNICATING)*

5. Distribute the remainder of materials and have the students set up growth mediums according to the following conditions (with upper grades, have pupils suggest their own conditions to be tested):

Specimen	Substance	Moisture	Temperature	Lightness
1	bread	dry	room	light
2	bread	dry	room	dark
3	bread	wet	room	light
4	bread	wet	room	dark
5	bread	dry	cold	light
6	bread	dry	cold	dark
7	bread	wet	cold	light
8	bread	wet	cold	dark

Place a piece of bread in each baby food jar. Use the eyedropper to add water if necessary.

Note: The same experiment can be done for a nonliving specimen, such as stone. Also, the number of variables can be reduced for simpler studies.

6. Have each group record (a) the specimens and conditions, (b) the beginning date, (c) the date of the first sign of growth, (d) the amount of growth from daily observations, and (e) periodic drawings of the growth.

7. Discuss the results. (Refer to the Conclusion.)
"Which specimens showed mold growth?"
"Which did not?" "Why do you think they didn't?"
"What conditions caused the mold to grow the most?"
(CLASSIFYING, INFERRING, COMMUNICATING)

Conclusion
Molds need substances with moisture and a source of food in order to grow. Moisture, warmth, and darkness increase the rate of growth.

Follow-up Activities
1. Have students test other host specimens and conditions.
2. Direct students to collect various kinds of mold specimens from inside and outside their homes. What similarities or differences in the specimens can they discover?

CREEPING AND CRAWLING

| KITS NEEDED: | **Kit 1, 2** | GRADE LEVEL: | **5–6** |

| SUGGESTED TIME: | One 50-minute period, followed by periodic observations |

Introduction
Although the sight of a crawling earthworm may cause some to shy away, the benefits this lowly creature provides for humans far outweigh any feelings of revulsion. Not only are earthworms a valuable food source for many animals, but, because of their presence in the soil, humans are able to produce better crops.

Organization and Materials
This activity is best suited for groups of three or four students.

Per Group: Large jar, can, soil, five earthworms, container of water, construction paper, balance scale, ruler, paper, pencils.

Procedure
1. Have students prepare "worm observation labs" by placing a tin can upright in the center of each jar. Tell students to record the weight of the soil before placing it in the space between the can and the jar to a height equal to the top of the can.
2. Direct students to place the worms on the construction paper. Have the students observe the worms, noting their apparent lack of physical characteristics.
"How do you think a worm eats?"
(INFERRING, OBSERVING)
3. Have students dip the worms in a container of water, place them back on the construction paper, and observe the paths created by the movement of the worms.
"What advantages are there for the worm to move in this manner?" (The worm covers more area this way.)   *(INFERRING, OBSERVING)*
4. Have students measure each worm and draw a picture of it.

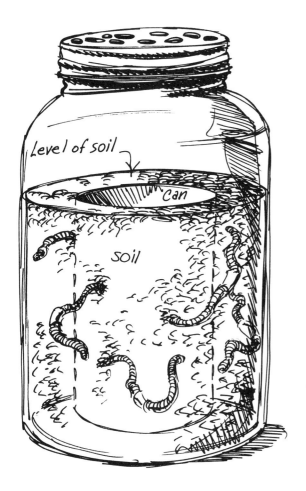

Level of soil

Can

soil

5. Tell students to place the worms into the soil and wrap dark construction paper around the outside of the jar. Direct them to cover the jar and let it stand until the next day.

"Why would it be helpful to cover the jar with dark paper?" (This simulates the darkness found in the worm's natural environment.)
(INFERRING)

6. Have students remove the paper each day and observe any changes in the soil.   *(OBSERVING)*

7. After two weeks of observations, instruct students to remove and measure the worms again. They should also weigh the soil and compare the measurements with those taken previously.

"How have the worms changed?"

"How has the weight or consistency of the soil changed?"

(OBSERVING, EXPERIMENTING, MEASURING)

8. Release the worms outside in an area containing soil.

Conclusion

Worms feed by taking soil through their bodies, creating tunnels as they go. These tunnels allow for better aeration of the soil, providing plants with the oxygen they need for growth.

Follow-up Activities

1. Have students construct a large observation lab (an aquarium or terrarium) where worms can be observed over a long period. Direct students to record growth rates, reproduction rates, and soil changes.

2. Provide several different soil conditions in which the worms can live (sand, clay, humus). Have students record the worms' adaptability to each.

FEATHERED FRIENDS

KITS NEEDED: **Kits 1, 2, 3** GRADE LEVEL: **4—5**

SUGGESTED TIME: Three 50-minute periods, followed by periodic observations

Introduction

Birds give us a great deal of pleasure with their beauty and song. These aren't the only benefits we gain from our feathered friends, though. By closely observing the local bird population, students can gain increased knowledge and appreciation of birds' relation to humans.

Organization and Materials

This activity is best suited as a class project, with certain aspects handled by smaller groups.

Per Class: Construction paper, plastic milk cartons, birdseed, pine cones, crayons, peanut butter, string.

Procedure

1. Locate an outdoor area near your school that lends itself to attracting birds.

2. Have students cut a rectangular section out of the side of a plastic milk carton, leaving at least a two-inch border of plastic around the bottom. Instruct them to fill the container with birdseed and hang it in the outdoor area.

"How can we change the appearance of the feeder to better blend into the surroundings?" (Glue leaves on the container, paint the container, and so on.)

"Why would we want to do that?" (So birds will be attracted to it.) *(INFERRING)*

3. Have students mix the peanut butter with birdseed and insert the mixture into the hollow sections of the pine cones. They should tie a piece a string to each pine cone and hang them in the observation area.

4. Establish a time schedule whereby the students can observe the birds attracted to the observation area. If possible, arrange for the students to observe at the same time each day.

"Why would it be to our advantage to observe the birds at the same time each day?" *(INFERRING)*

5. While observing the birds at the feeding station, have students: (a) Draw pictures of the various birds. (b) Record the number of birds entering the area. (c) Note the number of different species of birds seen.

"How do different birds obtain their food?"

"Which birds seem to prefer one food over another?"

"What advantages might humans derive from these and other birds?" (Birds provide us with beauty and song. They also help to control insects.) *(OBSERVING, INFERRING)*

6. Continue to maintain the feeding station throughout the year. Have students record any changes in either the number or types of birds observed. *(OBSERVING)*

7. Have students develop graphs that record the number of birds seen in relation to the seasons of the year.

"Why are more birds seen during one season than another?" *(INFERRING)*

Conclusion

Ornithology, or the study of birds, can be a fascinating subject for students. Pupils gain an appreciation for the different species of birds native to their part of the country as well as an understanding of some of the birds' habits. The appearance and behavior of birds reflect not only climatic conditions but also the effects of adaptation and evolution.

Follow-up Activities

1. Have students construct a wall chart showing the various birds living in your area. They can include the information gathered from their observations.

2. Have students research the migratory patterns of birds and relate their findings to the data they have already gathered.

MEALWORM MAGIC

KITS NEEDED: **Kit 1, 2, 3**   GRADE LEVEL: **4—6**

SUGGESTED TIME: Two 50-minute periods

Introduction

Mealworms are the larval stage of the darkling beetle. As mealworms develop, they undergo a complete metamorphosis (egg, larva, pupa, beetle). Their life cycle is influenced to a great extent by temperature, with cooler temperatures delaying their development.

Mealworms provide students with an opportunity to study animal behavior. This investigation is divided into two distinct parts, which should be performed in succession. Part I introduces students to the mealworm and its characteristics through the use of observation, measurement, and communication skills. Part II is an unstructured activity allowing students to work independently, devising experiments, collecting data, and drawing conclusions while discovering how animals react to various conditions.

Materials

Per Student: One mealworm (mealworms may be purchased inexpensively at most pet stores), a ruler, a magnifying glass, a toothpick (to examine and move the mealworm), drawing paper, a mealworm home (plastic container with holes in the lid, a layer of bran, oats, or cornflakes, and a slice of apple to provide moisture), plus various other materials as determined by student investigations in Part II.

Procedure

PART I

1. Instruct students to spend time observing their mealworm using the magnifying glass, toothpick, and ruler. Have them list the characteristics they observe. Stress that the mealworms should be observed carefully so as not to harm them in any way.

(OBSERVING, MEASURING, COMMUNICATING)

2. Discuss the students' observations.

"What did you find out about your mealworm?" (Allow time for students to examine their mealworms as characteristics are discussed. Possible observations are: size, feel, color, smell, and physical features—eyes, mouth, ears, antennae, legs, body structure, and so on.)

"How does it move?"
(COMMUNICATING, OBSERVING)

3. After the students have had ample time to observe and discuss the characteristics of their mealworms, have each one draw a picture of his or her specimen. *(COMMUNICATING, MEASURING)*

PART II
This activity deals with how mealworms react to various conditions as investigated by the students.

1. "What else would you like to learn about your mealworms?" Accept student suggestions and discuss methods of investigating these characteristics. List five to ten of the suggestions on the board. Allow students to select one of the suggested investigations. *(COMMUNICATING)*

2. Possible investigations include:

"Do the mealworms prefer light over dark, one color over another, hot over cold? Do they prefer crumbled cornflakes, bran flakes, sugar, bread, or apple as food?"

"How do mealworms react to various substances, such as vinegar, alcohol, water, or milk?" (Drops of these substances should be placed next to each mealworm.) "How do they react to touch by various objects?"

"How far does the mealworm move in one minute under varying surface conditions—smooth, rough, warm, cold, lumpy, and so on?"

"Does the mealworm move in a straight line? Can a pattern be traced?"

"How does the mealworm move when placed in an empty box?"

These activities are only suggestions. Students should be allowed to formulate their own experiments as long as they do not harm the mealworms. Step-by-step procedures have been deliberately omitted, since we are striving to encourage development of problem-solving, data collection, interpretation, and evaluation skills in this activity.

3. As students perform their experiments, have them record conditions and results, which can be discussed when the experiments are concluded.

Conclusion
In both parts of this activity, the focus is not the factual information gathered but rather the development of measuring, observing, communicating, investigating, and problem-solving skills.

Follow-up Activities
1. Have students construct bar graphs and tables depicting mealworm reactions, sizes, and so on.
2. Direct students to study the growth of the mealworms and their life cycle over time.

SPEED IT UP!

KITS NEEDED:	**Kit 3**	GRADE LEVEL:	**4–6**

SUGGESTED TIME: One or two 50-minute periods

Introduction

We don't often think about our respiration or circulation, yet they are vital to our functioning and survival. In this activity, students will learn something about how these physiological actions operate with respect to their own bodies. Students will count, record, and compare their breaths and heartbeats both before and after vigorous exercise. They will then determine the time required to return to normal respiration and pulse. (Parts I and II may be done together or independently.)

Organization and Materials

Divide the class into groups of three.

Per Group: Three three-by-ten-centimeter strips of tissue, a clock or watch with a second hand.

Procedure

1. Have students perform a vigorous physical activity (step-ups, jumping jacks, running in place) for thirty to forty-five seconds and discuss how their bodies reacted (breathed harder, heart beat faster, legs hurt).
(OBSERVING, COMMUNICATING)

2. Have the students rest for two to three minutes while you explain that they are going to investigate how fast they breathe and how fast their heart beats before and after exercise.

PART I

1. Demonstrate how to record the number of breaths per minute: (a) Have Student 1 place one end of the tissue strip on the tip of his or her nose so the other end of the strip extends over the mouth. (b) Instruct Student 1 to breathe normally with his or her mouth open. (c) Student 2 acts as the timer. (d) Student 3 counts the number of breaths in one minute by noting the number of times the tissue is blown. (e) Have each student record the number of breaths per minute he or she makes. (More advanced classes may perform additional trials and determine an average.)
(OBSERVING, MEASURING, COMMUNICATING)

2. Repeat Step 1 immediately after the students (one by one) take part in vigorous exercise for thirty to forty-five seconds. Have students record breaths per minute at one-minute intervals until breathing returns to normal.
(OBSERVING, MEASURING, COMMUNICATING)

3. Compare and discuss the results.

"How many times did you breathe per minute before exercising?"

"Did everyone breathe the same number of times per minute?" (No)

"Why do you think we breathe differently?" (Some work harder than others; some are in better physical condition.)

"How long did it take for your breathing to return to normal?" (Answers will vary.)

"Why is it necessary for the body to breathe faster after exercise?"

"Do athletes (such as long-distance runners) have different rates of respiration than you do?" "Why?" (Conditioning.)
(COMMUNICATING, CLASSIFYING, INFERRING)

PART II

1. Demonstrate how to count the number of times the human heart beats in one minute by locating and counting pulse beats. (*Note:* Do not have students use their thumbs to feel for a pulse since thumbs have a faint pulse themselves.)

2. Allow students time to practice locating and counting their pulses. *(MEASURING)*

3. Have students count and record their pulse beats in one minute. Have one student time, one count his or her pulse beats, and the third student record. *(MEASURING, COMMUNICATING)*

4. Repeat the count after students take part in vigorous exercise for thirty to forty-five seconds. Record pulse beats per minute at one-minute intervals until pulse returns to normal.
(MEASURING, COMMUNICATING)

5. Compare and discuss results.

"How long did it take for your pulse rate to return to normal?" (Answers will vary.)

"Which increased the most, your breathing or your pulse rate?"

"Why do you think this was so?"

"Which returned to normal first?"

"Why does your heart beat faster after exercise?" (Various parts of the body need more oxygen, which is received from circulating blood.)

"Do athletes (such as long-distance runners) have different heart rates than you do?" "Why?" (Conditioning.) *(COMMUNICATING, INFERRING)*

Conclusion

Breathing and pulse rate increase as one exercises. The lungs must take in more oxygen to help one breathe, while the heart is required to work harder to pump blood to the various parts of the body.

Follow-up Activities

1. Have students perform additional trials and determine averages.

2. Direct students to measure their breathing and pulse rates when lying down, standing, and so on.

Physical Science
A C T I V I T I E S

From the time we get up in the morning until we climb back into bed at night, our lives are influenced by a countless variety of scientific laws and principles. Although we may give little thought to the soap floating in the bathtub, the static electricity in the carpet, or the mechanical can opener on the kitchen counter, they are all governed by basic tenets of science. The need to understand the forces that regulate our lives underscores the importance of physical science.

In this section your students will learn about simple machines such as pulleys, levers, and inclined planes. They will examine the laws of physics as they apply to color formation, static electricity, vibrations, force, and inertia. Students will also explore such scientific prerequisites as measuring and classifying. Finally, discoveries on the nature of fingerprints and the magic of magnets will open their eyes to the fascination of science.

Understanding our world means understanding the forces that influence it. As students explore the dimensions of their physical world through the processes of science, their curiosity will be aroused and their interest stimulated. In turn, they will develop a deeper appreciation for the physical principles and precepts of nature and learn to work in harmony with these precepts.

THE PLANE FACTS

KITS NEEDED: **Kit 1, 2**   GRADE LEVEL: **4-5**

SUGGESTED TIME: One 50-minute period

Introduction

Moving heavy objects from one level to another is a common problem. Whether the task is unloading boxes from a truck or moving a wheelchair from one floor to another, the use of ramps or inclined planes makes the job much easier. Using a plane increases the distance the object must be moved while decreasing the amount of force necessary for its movement.

Organization and Materials

This activity is best suited for groups of four or five students.

Per Group: One six-inch by three-foot piece of wood (measurements can vary), one chair, one spring scale, a string, two books.

Procedure

1. Tell students to tie the string around a book in a tight criss-cross manner.

2. Have students record the weight of the book as it hangs freely from the spring scale.
(MEASURING)

3. Direct students to place one end of the board on top of the seat of the chair, allowing the other end to rest on the floor, thus forming a ramp.

4. Instruct students to use the spring scale to pull the book up the ramp, recording its weight as they pull.

"Why does the weight of the book change as it goes up the ramp?" (The book is being moved over a longer distance.)

"How can you explain the difference in weight between holding and pulling the book?"
(INFERRING, OBSERVING)

5. Have students repeat the procedure using the same book balanced on end. They should record the results.

"What variable has changed in this trial?" (Area of the book, which affects friction.)

"How can you explain the difference in the force needed to move the on-end book up the ramp?" (Refer to the Conclusion.)
(INFERRING, COMMUNICATING)

6. Direct students to decrease the angle of the ramp by laying one end of the board on top of a book standing on end and resting the other end of the board on the floor.

7. Have the students pull the other book up this ramp using the spring scale, recording the book's weight as they pull.

"What factor do you think is responsible for the change in force necessary to pull the book up this new ramp?" *(INFERRING, COMMUNICATING)*

8. Instruct students to transfer the results of this experiment to the chart.

Conclusion

Using an inclined plane enables one to lessen the amount of force necessary to move an object. To benefit from this advantage, however, the distance that the object travels must be increased. Also, less surface area in contact with the inclined plane means less energy needed to move an object up the plane.

Follow-up Activities

1. Have students measure the distance the book travels relative to the amount of force necessary to move it over that distance; for example, how much force is necessary to move the book one foot compared with the force necessary to move it three feet. Ask them to conduct different experiments and chart the results.

2. Have students repeat Step 4 altering the surface of the board. (*Hint:* Suggest putting waxed paper on the surface or putting round pencils under the book.) They should record the changes.

YOU'RE IN MY SPACE

KITS NEEDED: **Kit 2, 3**   GRADE LEVEL: **4—5**

SUGGESTED TIME: One 50-minute period

Introduction

All states of matter (solids, liquids, and gases) occupy three dimensions and thus can be measured in volume. Although all three may differ in weight, density, and physical characteristics, they are similar in that each takes up space—but never the same space at the same time.

Organization and Materials

This activity is best suited for groups of three to four students.

Per Group: One coffee can, some clay, a plastic straw, several large corks, three balloons, some large stones (able to fit into the cans), a string, one test tube, water, crayon.

Procedure

1. Using a sharp object, puncture a hole the width of a straw in the side of each coffee can exactly two inches from the top of the can.

2. Have students cut a two-inch section of straw and insert it into the hole in their can, securing the straw with a piece of clay. (*Hint:* Precutting the straws on an angle will expedite the activity.)

3. Have each group calibrate the test tube using a wax crayon.

"Why is it important for us to mark the test tube in equal segments?" (All variables must be controlled.) *(INFERRING, MEASURING)*

4. Direct students to push the test tube bottom into a small ball of clay and position it under the end of the straw outside the can.

5. Tell students to fill the can with water until water flows from the straw.

"By filling the can to its overflow point, what does this assure us of?" (Equal amounts of water will be in each can.) *(INFERRING, EXPERIMENTING)*

7. Have the students blow up the three balloons to different sizes, each able to fit into the can.

"Can you predict which balloon will displace the most and which the least amount of water? Why?" *(PREDICTING, INFERRING)*

8. Instruct each group to force one balloon at a time into the can, recording the amount of water each displaces. (They will need to refill the can with water after each trial.)

"What is responsible for the different amounts of water being displaced?" (The size of the objects.)

"Would balloons of different shapes yield different results?"

(INFERRING, EXPERIMENTING, MEASURING)

9. Have the students record the information on a chart. *(COMMUNICATING, MEASURING)*

Conclusion

Although both the weight and shape of an object would seem to indicate its potential for occupying space, the only factor responsible for determining the amount of space an object takes is its volume.

Follow-up Activities

1. Have the students repeat Step 6 comparing the weights of the objects to their ability to displace water.

2. Have students repeat the activity using solutions other than water (salt water, sugar water, milk shake, and so on).

6. Have students begin lowering corks and stones into the water, noting on the test tube the amount of water each displaces. After each object has been removed from the can, the water level must be restored according to Step 5, and the test tube emptied. This procedure should be repeated two times for each object.

"Does the weight of the object seem to affect the amount of water it displaces?"

"Does the amount of time the object is kept under the water affect its ability for displacement?"

(EXPERIMENTING, MEASURING, OBSERVING)

WATER BABIES

KITS NEEDED: **Kit 1, 2, 3**   GRADE LEVEL: **4—6**

SUGGESTED TIME: One 50-minute period

Introduction

The ability of water to support an object is determined by the weight of the water the object displaces. This principle allows a large metal ship to float yet causes a small pebble to sink.

Organization and Materials

This activity is best suited for groups of three or four students.

Per Group: Six-inch by six-inch piece of aluminum foil, one large jar or can, several paper clips, cork, pencil, crayon, twenty pennies.

Procedure

1. Pass out all materials and have students list objects to be tested on one of the charts in the appendix. Also, have each group record their prediction as to whether each object will float or sink. *(PREDICTING)*

2. Have students fill the large jar with water to within two inches of the top.

3. Direct students to place objects into the water one by one and record the results.

"List several possibilities as to why some objects float while others do not." (Weight, shape, composition.) *(INFERRING, EXPERIMENTING)*

4. Tell students to tear a piece approximately two inches by two inches from the square of aluminum foil and tightly squeeze the foil to form a small, hard ball.

"What do you think will happen to the ball of foil when it is dropped into the water?" *(PREDICTING)*

5. Have students drop the ball into the water and record the results. *(OBSERVING)*

6. Using the remaining piece of foil, have each group construct a boatlike structure consisting of a base and four sides.

"What will happen when you set the boat on the water?" "Why?" *(INFERRING, PREDICTING)*

7. Direct students to carefully set the boat on the water and slowly add pennies to it. Record the total number of pennies each group puts in their boat before the boat tips or sinks.

"Why did the larger piece of aluminum float while the smaller one sank?" (Refer to the Conclusion.) *(INFERRING)*

Conclusion

Water has the ability to keep certain objects afloat. This ability depends on the volume of water displaced in relation to the weight of the object.

Follow-up Activities

1. Have the students construct several aluminum boats of various sizes and shapes. Each can be tested for its ability to support weight.

2. Through testing and observation, have students identify those materials best suited for the building of a ship. If possible, provide opportunities for students to build and test their ideas.

STONE SOUP

KITS NEEDED: **Kit 1, 2, 3**   GRADE LEVEL: **4−6**

SUGGESTED TIME: One 50-minute period

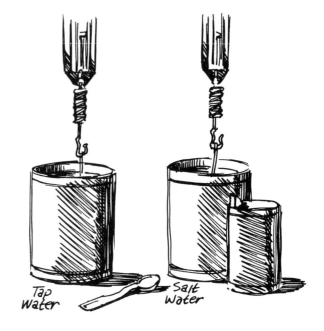

Tap Water   Salt Water

Introduction

The upward push of water causes some materials to float and others to weigh less when submerged. The density, or thickness of the water, determines the amount of push it is capable of providing.

Organization and Materials

This activity is suited for groups of three to four students.

Per Group: Two coffee cans, some string, a spring scale, some salt, a spoon, three different-sized stones.

Procedure

1. Have each group fill their cans with water to within two inches of the top.

2. Instruct students to tie a piece of string to each of the stones and to weigh the stones one at a time by tying the other end of the string to the spring scale.

3. Have students record the weights of the three stones.

"Does the size of the stone seem to affect its weight?" "How?"   *(MEASURING, INFERRING)*

4. Have students submerge each stone in the water and record the new weights. (The stones should not touch bottom.)

"What can we conclude about the weight of an object submerged in water?" (The weight decreases.)   *(INFERRING)*

5. Have students add salt to the water in one of the cans, stirring until the water is saturated.

6. Repeat Step 4 using the salt water. Record the results.

"How can you explain the difference in the weights of the stones submerged in the two types of water?" (Refer to the Conclusion.)
(INFERRING)

Conclusion

The density of a liquid determines the amount of force it is able to exert upward on an object. Because salt water is thicker than tap water, it pushes upward with a greater force.

Follow-up Activities

1. Using the two solutions prepared for this activity, have the students check other materials for buoyancy. (*Hint:* An egg demonstrates this principle very well.)

2. Have students attempt to graph the buoyancy of other liquids, such as paint or molasses, using a single weight as a constant.

A PRESSING FACT

| KITS NEEDED: | **Kit 2, 3** | GRADE LEVEL: | **4−6** |

| SUGGESTED TIME: | One 50-minute period |

Paper towel

Introduction
Air is a substance that takes up space and has weight. Although this fact is not easily seen, it can be demonstrated with the following experiment.

Organization and Materials
This project can be done initially as a demonstration. The class can then be divided into groups of two to four to experiment on their own.

Per Group: One large container in which to put water (such as a five-gallon aquarium or a large bucket), one clear glass, several dry tissues or paper towels, one cork.

Procedure
1. Place at least eight inches of water in a large container. *(MEASURING)*
2. Push a dry paper towel into a dry glass.
"What do you think will happen if we push the glass under the water?" *(PREDICTING)*
"Why is it important for the entire towel to be inside the glass?" (The accuracy of the activity depends on this.) *(OBSERVING, INFERRING)*
3. Holding the glass upside down, push it under the water. *(EXPERIMENTING)*
"Why must the glass enter the water with the top horizontal to the water?" (To prevent water from displacing the air inside the glass.)
(INFERRING)
4. Remove the glass and allow students to inspect the paper towel. *(OBSERVING)*
5. Discuss results with the students.
(COMMUNICATING)
"What do you notice about the paper towel?"
(OBSERVING)
"Why do you think the towel remained dry?"
(The air pressure kept the water out.)
(INFERRING)
How long could the glass remain under the water without the towel getting wet?" "Why?"
"Would the towel stay dry if the glass was submerged at different angles?" (No.)
(EXPERIMENTING, INFERRING)

6. Remove the paper towel from the glass and float a cork in the large container.
(EXPERIMENTING)
7. Ask the class to predict what will occur when the glass is placed over the cork and submerged.
(PREDICTING)
8. Discuss results with the class.
"Why did the cork behave the way it did?" (The air pressure forced the cork as well as the water.)
"Would the cork ever travel up the trapped air inside the glass?" *(COMMUNICATING)*

Conclusion
No two substances can occupy the same space at the same time. As long as air occupied the space inside the glass, no water was able to enter—thus keeping the paper towel dry and pushing the cork to the bottom of the large container.

Follow-up Activities
1. Have students complete the activity using other materials that float.
2. Have students conduct the activity using liquids of different density (vinegar, salad oil, rubbing alcohol, orange juice, and so on). It may be necessary to reduce the quantity of a chosen liquid as well as the size of the other materials. Ask students to predict whether the results will be the same for all liquids.

HEAT IT UP

KITS NEEDED: **Kit 1, 3**   **GRADE LEVEL:** **4−6**

SUGGESTED TIME: One 50-minute period

Introduction

The movement of heat through material is called conduction. When atoms (or molecules) are heated, they vibrate faster and faster, striking neighboring atoms. These atoms, in turn, strike adjoining atoms. In this way, heat travels from one end of an object to another.

Organization and Materials

Because this experiment uses fire, it is advisable for the teacher to conduct it as a demonstration, with the class assisting up to the point of lighting the candle.

Six paper clips, a watch with a second hand, seventeen inches of bare copper wire, one candle, modeling clay, one piece of aluminum foil, stopwatch.

Procedure

1. Bend the copper wire and insert both ends into the clay (see drawing).
2. Melt some wax onto a piece of aluminum foil. This wax should be soft enough to use for the next step.
3. Hang the paper clips about one inch apart along the wire, attaching them with the wax.

"Why don't we hang the paper clips at varying distances?"   *(INFERRING)*

"What would be the effect of hanging the clips at two-inch intervals, rather than one-inch intervals?" (It would take longer to heat each clip.) *(INFERRING)*

4. Place the lighted candle at one end of the wire so the flame touches the wire.   *(EXPERIMENTING)*

5. Time the intervals between the dropping paper clips.

"Why is it important to be accurate in timing these intervals?" (Accurate measurements are necessary for reliable results.)   *(MEASURING)*

6. Have students record the results by creating a bar graph.   *(MEASURING, EXPERIMENTING)*

Conclusion

As the atoms or molecules in the copper wire are heated, their movement increases, causing them to bump into each other. This chain reaction steadily continues away from the heat source. The farther the clips are from the heat source, the longer it takes for the heat to reach them.

Follow-up Activities

1. Complete this experiment using other types of wire and compare times. The difference in times will show the ability of the wire to be a conductor.
2. Repeat this experiment using two candles placed at opposite ends of the wire. Have students record the results.

1-2-3 PULL!

KITS NEEDED:	**Kit 1, 2, 3**	GRADE LEVEL: **4—5**

SUGGESTED TIME:	Two 50-minute periods

Yogurt lid

Introduction

When one object moves across another, friction is created. Various surfaces help or hinder the movement of one object across another. Students use manipulative, measurement, and recording skills as they construct a device to move a load across a given surface.

Organization and Materials

Groups of three to four students are necessary for this activity.

Per Group: One yogurt container and lid, tape, a plastic or paper cup, water, one piece of string (sixty centimeters long), twenty pennies, various surfaces (rough wood, carpet, sandpaper, styrofoam, tin foil, construction paper—whatever is available).

Procedure

1. Direct students to cover a desk surface with construction paper and mark off a starting point in the middle of the desk.

2. Have the students securely tape one end of the string to the yogurt lid and the other end to the yogurt container. The cup should be filled with approximately 80 millileters of water and placed on top of the lid at the starting point on the desk. (The amount of water should be adjusted as needed to counterbalance the weight of the yogurt container when it is suspended over the side of the table.) *(MEASURING)*

3. "How can we move our water-loaded lid to the edge of the desk?" (Accept all answers.) *(COMMUNICATING)*

4. "How many pennies placed in the yogurt container do you think it will take to move the lid to the end of the desk? Record your prediction." *(PREDICTING, COMMUNICATING)*

5. Have the students place pennies (one by one) in the container until the lid moves all the way to the end of the desk. Record the results. (For older students, a system can be set up to measure the distance each weight causes the lid to move.) *(MEASURING, COMMUNICATING)*

6. "How can we move the water-loaded lid more easily with fewer pennies?" (Accept all hypotheses.) *(INFERRING, COMMUNICATING)*

7. Discuss the various surfaces you have available and have the students predict how many pennies will be needed to move the lid to the edge of the desk and record their predictions. *(COMMUNICATING, PREDICTING)*

8. Allow the students to test their hypotheses and record their results. *(EXPERIMENTING, COMMUNICATING)*

9. Discuss the results. *(COMMUNICATING)*

10. "Why and where might rougher surfaces be used to slow down movement?"

"Can you think of other places rough surfaces are used?" (Bathtubs, locker room floors, stairs.) *(COMMUNICATING, INFERRING)*

Conclusion
Objects move more easily over smoother surfaces than they do over rough surfaces. This is because there is less friction on smoother surfaces.

Follow-up Activities
1. Have students measure the distance the lid moves each time a penny is added to the cup.
2. Challenge students to devise a surface that will allow a given object to move a specified distance using a given number of pennies (students may combine surfaces).
3. Restrict students to the use of one type of surface and have them discover ways to make the lid move more easily (students may alter the surface of the material—wax it, wet it, and so on).

SWING FAST, SWING SLOW

KITS NEEDED: **Kit 1, 2, 3**   GRADE LEVEL: **5—6**

SUGGESTED TIME: **One 50-minute period**

Introduction
The length of a pendulum arm affects the speed of a pendulum. As the length of the arm increases, the speed of the pendulum decreases. Conversely, as the length of the pendulum arm is shortened, the speed of the arm increases.

Organization and Materials
Each group should have two students.

Per Group: One thirty-inch piece of string, pendulum weights (washers, nuts, or paper clips), ruler, stopwatch or watch with a second hand.

Procedure
1. Discuss what a pendulum is and how it is used. *(COMMUNICATION)*
2. Demonstrate how to construct a pendulum (slip a weight over one end of a string and fold the string in half).
3. Make sure the length of the string is ten inches, and wrap the excess around your hand.
4. Hold the string between your thumb and forefinger. With the other hand, hold the weight at any angle and ask the students to predict how many times the pendulum will make a complete swing (back and forth) in thirty seconds. Record the predictions on the board. Let go of the weight and have students count the number of swings. *(OBSERVING, PREDICTING, COMMUNICATING)*
5. Distribute the materials and have the students set up their own pendulums.
6. Have students in each group perform two trials and record the results. *(EXPERIMENTING, COMMUNICATING)*

7. "How could we change the number of swings of the pendulum arm in thirty seconds?" List the various hypotheses on the board.
(INFERRING, COMMUNICATING)

8. Have the students test the various hypotheses one by one by (a) listing each hypothesis or changed condition on their chart, (b) making and recording predictions for each condition, and (c) testing and recording the results of each trial.
(PREDICTING, EXPERIMENTING, MEASURING, COMMUNICATING)

9. Discuss the results.

Conclusion

The length of a pendulum affects the number of swings (speed) in a given time period. A shorter arc produces a faster swing and hence more swings. A longer arm produces a slower swing and fewer swings.

Follow-up Activities

1. Have students construct a graph indicating how the length of the pendulum arm affects the swing of the arm.

2. A specified number of trials may be performed for each condition, leading students to arrive at an average for each of several conditions.

3. Stationary pendulums could be constructed and collision reactions between pairs observed and measured.

4. Have students determine a way to measure the length of the arc of the swing using graph paper.

5. Have students predict and investigate how long (in minutes or seconds) the pendulum arm will swing.

JUST STRUMMING ALONG

KITS NEEDED: **Kit 2**		GRADE LEVEL: **4—6**
SUGGESTED TIME:	One 50-minute period	

Introduction

The speed at which an object vibrates determines the pitch of the sound it produces. By and large, when an object vibrates rapidly it produces a higher-pitched sound than when it vibrates slowly.

Organization and Materials

Students can work individually or in groups of two.

Per Group: One plastic ruler.

Procedure

1. "Can anyone explain how to make a sound with this ruler?" (Have students demonstrate their answers.) *(COMMUNICATING)*

2. Have the students strum their rulers by placing part of the ruler on the desk and flicking the end that extends out from the desk, making sure to hold the other end firmly. "Besides the sound produced, what else do you observe?" (The ruler vibrates.) *(OBSERVING, COMMUNICATING)*

3. Instruct students to place the rulers so that the twenty-centimeter mark is at the edge of the desk (the one-centimeter mark should extend over the edge of the desk). *(MEASURING)*

4. Have the students flick the end of the ruler.

"How do you know the ruler is moving (vibrating)?" (Students will be able to see the vibrations better if they crouch down even with the edge of the ruler.)

"Describe the movement (vibration)."
(OBSERVING, COMMUNICATING)

5. "Now place the fourteen-centimeter mark at the edge of the desk and flick the ruler again." (Instruct students to try to flick the ruler with the same force each time.)

"What do you observe about the movement (vibration) of the ruler?" (The ruler is moving faster; it is becoming more difficult to see the double image.)

Students may want to try the twenty-five-centimeter mark for comparison.
(OBSERVING, EXPERIMENTING)

6. "What other differences did you notice?" (The sound is different.) *(COMMUNICATING)*

7. Allow students to experiment with their rulers beginning at the twenty-centimeter mark and moving the ruler two centimeters thereafter, recording (a) the centimeter mark, (b) the speed of the movement (vibration) in comparison to the previous trial, and (c) the sound made in comparison to the previous trial.

Example: "20 cm—slow—low; 18 cm—faster—higher; 16 cm—faster—higher."
(EXPERIMENTING, MEASURING, OBSERVING)

8. "What did you conclude?" (Have the students demonstrate to support their conclusions.)
(INFERRING, COMMUNICATING)

Conclusion

The shorter the ruler, the faster it vibrates. An object vibrating at a higher speed produces a higher-pitched sound than an object vibrating at a slower speed.

Follow-up Activities

1. Have students test materials other than plastic, such as wood, metal, cardboard, or rubber bands.

2. Challenge students to produce various sounds.

3. Have students construct musical instruments using the vibration principle.

SOLVING MAGNETIC MYSTERIES

KITS NEEDED: **Kit 3**   GRADE LEVEL: **4—5**

SUGGESTED TIME: One 50-minute period

Introduction

We have all seen magnets sticking to refrigerators, stoves, some school blackboards, and other metallic objects. But why aren't all keys, which are made of metal, attracted to a magnet? In this activity, students will learn what kinds of materials (steel) are attracted to magnets.

Organization and Materials

This activity is appropriate for individuals, pairs, or small groups, depending on availability of materials.

Per Group: Magnets, various materials to be tested (emery cloth, plastic, steel foil, lead foil, waxed paper, paper clips, fur, aluminum foil, paper, brass foil, sponge squares of two different colors, and so on). In preparing the sponge squares, select one of the colors and hide steel pins (with points and heads cut off) inside. Be careful that the ends are not sticking out. Test to make sure that the sponges are attracted to a magnet. Have sponges available in sufficient quantities so that half of the class receives one color and the other half receives the color with the steel pins.

(*Note:* Foil squares and magnets are available from Delta Education, Box M, Nashua, N.H. 03061 at reasonable prices and in sufficient quantity for an entire class.)

Procedure

1. Conduct a brief discussion to determine what the students already know about magnets and magnetism. Students might be asked:

"Who can explain what this is?" (Magnet.)

"What do magnets do?" (They attract various objects.)

"What kinds of objects do magnets attract?" (Accept all answers for now and if disagreements arise, explain that students will discover the answers as the activity progresses.)

(COMMUNICATING)

2. Distribute materials to be tested and discuss the characteristics of each.

Note: All materials to be tested can be stored in large envelopes to make dispersal and collection easier.

(CLASSIFYING, COMMUNICATING, OBSERVING)

3. Instruct students to carefully examine the materials and predict which are magnetic.

(OBSERVING, INFERRING)

4. When all students have completed their predictions, class totals can be listed on the board. (This will serve to extend the recording process as well as help integrate math procedures into the experiment. For example, "If there are twenty-five students in the class and nineteen predicted that emery cloth is magnetic, how many predicted that it is not?")

(COMMUNICATING, MEASURING, CLASSIFYING)

5. Distribute the bar magnets and allow students to test their predictions. Have the students record their findings on a worksheet as they proceed. Have them use a mark that will differentiate the actual results from their predictions.

(EXPERIMENTING, OBSERVING, COMMUNICATING)

6. Results can be listed on the board as in Step 4, if desired.   *(COMMUNICATING)*

7. Discuss the findings with the class.

"Which materials were magnetic?"

"There seem to be some different findings as to whether sponges are magnetic. Can someone explain this?" (Students may decide that the color is the determining factor. If so, ask how this theory can be proven. One solution: Different colors of paper, plastic, cloth, or wood could be tested. This question could be left open to be explored in the follow-up activities. The purpose of the trick sponges is to challenge the students to use higher levels of thinking and to use a scientific approach to explaining unusual.)

"Can you think of other objects or materials that may be magnetic?"

(COMMUNICATING, CLASSIFYING, INFERRING, PREDICTING)

Conclusion

Materials must be made of or contain steel in order to be magnetic.

Follow-up Activities

1. Demonstrate a magnet picking up one pin but not another (steel versus aluminum).

"What is the problem here?" (One pin is not made of steel.)

"What does this show about whether an object is magnetic or not?" (It must be steel.)

2. Test the ability of magnetism to pass through the objects tested.

3. If possible, allow students to keep their bar magnets at their desk or on a table to investigate other materials.

4. Have the students list some of the ways magnets are used in our everyday world (refrigerator magnets, metallic weatherstripping for doors, cranes in junkyards, and so on).

YOU SHOCK ME!

KITS NEEDED: **Kit 3**	GRADE LEVEL: **4—5**

SUGGESTED TIME: One 50-minute period

Introduction

Your hair is uncontrollable and stands on end, your dress or slacks cling to your legs, your sweater crackles as you take it off, and the styrofoam packing pieces mysteriously fly all over as you unpack your book order. Static electricity is the cause of these unusual happenings. Students will learn that static electricity may be created by rubbing objects together, that it causes objects to attract or repel other objects, and that it may be removed from an object by rubbing it with certain other objects.

Organization and Materials

Students can work alone or in pairs.

Per Group: One inflated balloon for each student, a six-inch piece of string or yarn (attached to the inflated balloon).

Note: This activity should be conducted on cold, crisp days (low humidity). Caution students that static electricity experiments should not be tried with current electricity (outlets, lights, and so on).

Procedure

1. Introduce this activity with a discussion on electricity.

"What is electricity?"

"How is electricity used?"

"Where does electricity come from?"

Explain that there are two kinds of electricity: current electricity (the type used in our homes for light and electrical power) and static electricity (the type experienced when we receive a shock from touching another person).

(COMMUNICATING, INFERRING)

2. Supply each student with an inflated balloon. Have the students stand next to some object in the room (wall, chalkboard, door, window). Ask them to hold their balloons against the object and carefully let it go.

"What happens?" (The balloon falls to the floor.)

"Does anyone know how we can make the balloon stick to the object?" (From past experience students will probably suggest rubbing the balloon against something such as their hair, a sweater, a rug, and so on).

(OBSERVING, COMMUNICATING, EXPERIMENTING)

3. Have the students rub their balloons on their hair or clothing.

"Now hold the balloon against the wall (door, window) and let it go. What happens?" (The balloon sticks.)

"What caused the balloon to stick to the object this time?" (An in-depth scientific explanation is not necessary—"Rubbing it against my head" is sufficient.)

"How long will your balloon stay there?" (Allow an extra balloon to remain on the wall to observe as the activity continues.)

(OBSERVING, COMMUNICATING, EXPERIMENTING, INFERRING, PREDICTING, MEASURING)

4. Have the students remove their balloons from the wall and rub their hands over the entire balloon a couple of times.

"Now try to stick the balloon to the wall again. What happens?" (The balloon falls to the floor.)

"Can you explain this?" (The electrical charge was removed.)

"Does rubbing the balloon against your hands do the same thing to the balloon as rubbing it against your hair or sweater does?"

"What does this tell you?" (Not all objects cause a static charge when rubbed against each other.)

(OBSERVING, COMMUNICATING, INFERRING)

5. Have one student charge his or her balloon and hold it above the hair of another student.

"What happened? Is this similar to the balloon sticking to the wall?"

Allow all students to perform this trick.

6. Have all the students charge their balloons again. Have two students hold their balloons by the strings and bring them together.

"What happened?" (The balloons pushed apart.)

"Why do you think this happened?"

"What did we do differently this time?"

(EXPERIMENTING, OBSERVING, INFERRING)

7. Have students cite examples of other forms of static electricity they have experienced in their everyday lives. *(COMMUNICATING)*

Conclusion

Static electricity is caused by rubbing certain types of objects together. When an object is charged, it may attract or stick to other objects. When two like objects are charged, they push or repel each other. However, static electricity does not last long.

Follow-up Activities

1. Students can test materials besides balloons to see whether they can be charged to attract various objects.

2. Using strips of newspaper, have students place one strip on top of another and rub them with a pencil. Both strips should then be held between the forefinger and thumb. Have students observe and record the results. Repeat the activity, but have students place the strips side by side when rubbing.

COLORIFIC

KITS NEEDED:	**Kit 1**	GRADE LEVEL:	**4—6**
SUGGESTED TIME:		Two 50-minute periods	

Introduction

Color is everywhere. Clothing, homes, computers, billboards—all exhibit many beautiful colors. But where do these colors come from? All colors come from the spectrum of white light. When separated from white light these colors include red, yellow, and blue, the primary colors. The primary colors, when combined in various amounts, produce all the other colors around us.

Organization and Materials

This project is designed as a class demonstration, followed by individual work using the information obtained during the demonstration.

Per Class: A large piece of construction paper (white), colored cellophane (red, yellow, green, blue), two light projectors, tape.

Procedure

1. Hang the piece of white paper on the wall or chalkboard.

2. Have the students look at the white paper through individual pieces of colored cellophane and through overlapping colors of cellophane.

"What happens to the color of the white paper as you look at it?" (The color changes.)

(OBSERVING)

3. Darken the room.

4. With a light projector, shine a beam of light through the red cellophane onto the white paper.

"What color do you see on the white paper?" (Red.) *(OBSERVING)*

5. Continue this process with the other colors of cellophane. Have the students record the various colors on a chart. *(EXPERIMENTING, OBSERVING)*

6. Use tape to cover two light projectors, each with a different color of cellophane.

7. Shine the two lights together on the white paper. Ask students to record the results on a chart. Repeat this process with other colors of cellophane until all possible combinations are produced.

"What combinations produce the brightest colors?"

"What combinations produce completely new colors?"

"What combinations are most like primary colors?"

"Which ones are least like primary colors?"
(OBSERVING, EXPERIMENTING)

Conclusion
By analyzing the charts, students should be able to conclude that when the primary colors are mixed together in various combinations the secondary colors are produced.

Follow-up Activities
1. Provide red, blue, and yellow paint to allow students to create and experiment with the primary colors. (*Note:* Results may be somewhat different from results obtained by mixing light.)

2. Direct students to find a way, without using a prism, to separate the colors found in white light.

RAINBOW RACE
KITS NEEDED: **Kit 1, 2, 3**   GRADE LEVEL: **5—6**

SUGGESTED TIME: One 50-minute period

Introduction
Only one end of an alcohol burner's wick is in the alcohol, but the other end is also wet—the same would not happen if the wick was replaced with a popsicle stick. Certain materials permit liquids to permeate them. Students will observe the speed of various liquids moving up a strip of paper, over colored dots, breaking these colors apart and leaving behind a colorful path.

Organization and Materials
Students should work individually or in pairs.

For Display: One paper towel strip (six by twenty-five centimeters), one plastic cup or glass with four centimeters of water.

Per Group: At least two paper towel strips (six by twelve centimeters), three strips of spackling tape or blotter paper (six by twelve centimeters), a centimeter ruler, various water-soluble colored markers, water, two clear plastic cups or glasses, a timing device.

Procedure
1. Display a strip of paper towel with one end in a liquid (water) and the rest draped over the edge of the cup.

"How did the paper towel above the liquid get wet?" (A discussion of capillary action may be helpful at this time, depending on the age of the students.) *(INFERRING, COMMUNICATING)*

2. Have the students fold one of their paper towel strips in half, lengthwise.

3. Instruct students to use a colored marker to place a solid dot (about the size of a dime) on one side of the paper towel approximately five centimeters from the bottom. They should do the same on the other side of the fold using a different color. *(MEASURING)*

4. Direct students to pour two to three centimeters of water into a plastic glass. *(MEASURING)*

5. Tell students to place the dotted end of the paper into the cup and to record the starting time. *(COMMUNICATING)*

6. "What do you observe?" (Water begins to move up the strip.)
(OBSERVING, COMMUNICATING)

7. Have students record the time the water reaches the colored dots.
"How long did it take for the liquid to reach the dots?"
(OBSERVING, MEASURING, COMMUNICATING)

8. "What happened as the liquid passed over the colored dots?" (The dots began to spread over the strip in various colors.)
"Where do you think the various colors come from?" (A review of primary and secondary colors may be helpful.) *(OBSERVING, INFERRING)*

9. "What if we use a different kind of paper?" (Pass out strips of spackling tape and have the students examine it and predict how they think the liquid will travel up it.)
(OBSERVING, INFERRING, PREDICTING)

10. Have students set up another trial (repeat steps 3 through 8) using the spackling tape instead of the paper towel.

11. "How fast does the water travel up the spackling tape as compared to the paper towel?"
"What do you think causes the difference?"
(OBSERVING, MEASURING, INFERRING)

12. "Can you think of any other factors that may affect the speed the liquid moves?"

Conclusion

The composition of the paper affects the speed that the water moves up a strip of material. As the liquid moves over the colored dots, it separates the colors into their component colors.

Follow-up Activities

1. Have students try other kinds of paper and compare results to those for the paper towel and spackling tape.

2. Have students test other factors that may affect the speed of capillary movement (the type of liquid, various types of colors—crayons, pens, food coloring, and so on).

SWIRLS AND WHORLS

KITS NEEDED: **Kit 1, 2**   GRADE LEVEL: **4—6**

SUGGESTED TIME: Two 50-minute periods

Introduction
Students can fine-tune their observational skills as they study the individuality of fingerprints. Although similarities do exist from one set of prints to another, no two sets are ever exactly alike.

Organization and Materials
This activity is best completed individually by each student.

Per Student: One three-by-five index card, one sheet of plain paper, five one-inch pieces of cellophane tape, one magnifying glass, a pencil.

Procedure
1. Give each student a plain piece of paper and a three-by-five card. Have each student lightly print his or her name on the back of each.
2. Have each student use the side of a pencil to color a dark area (approximately two inches by two inches) at the top of the plain white paper.
3. Have each student apply pressure to the colored area using the right index finger.
4. Being careful not to smudge the colored finger, have each student slowly press a piece of cellophane tape against the finger, remove the tape, and place the tape on the plain side of the index card, leaving room for the other four fingerprints.
5. Have students repeat this procedure with the other fingers of the right hand. (*Hint:* In between fingers, have students recolor the pencilled area.)

"Is there anything unique or unusual about your fingerprints?"   (*OBSERVING*)

6. Collect all the cards. Divide the class into groups of eight to twelve and pass out a card and magnifying lens to each person in the group. Have each group examine the cards and place them into piles exhibiting similar characteristics.

"Does any one pattern appear more often than others?"

"How many different patterns do you see?" (*OBSERVING, CLASSIFYING*)

7. Display all the index cards in the front of the classroom. Have each student select one card and match fingerprints to an individual in the room. After all the cards have been assigned, check the names on the backs.

"What special characteristics did you note on your card?"   (*COMMUNICATING*)

Conclusion
Although there may be only three or four basic fingerprint patterns, there are a countless number of irregularities that distinguish any one pattern from all others.

Follow-up Activities
1. Have students expand this activity to include several other classes.
2. Ask students to research the patterns of people of different ages. Students may then report their findings, making generalizations concerning each age group along with possible reasons for differences observed.
3. Students may wish to construct a class scrapbook of fingerprints, organized into different categories (patterns).

Earth Science
 A C T I V I T I E S

Four and a half billion. It's a number almost too large to comprehend. Yet that's how many years the Earth has been in existence. During that time it has undergone some remarkable changes. Rocks have formed, primeval seas have ebbed and flowed across vast continents, and dramatic weather conditions have contributed to the geography and structure of our planet. Still, it's amazing to realize that this planet is only a microcosm in the vastness of the universe. It is but one particle in a galaxy of stars, satellites, meteorites, and other celestial bodies. The beauty of our world and its place in the universe are areas ripe for exploration.

Knowledge of our world contributes not only to an appreciation of its existence but to an initiative to preserve it as well.

In this section students learn about the geology of the Earth—its rocks, sand, and soil—and about how the forces of nature contribute to erosion, the Earth's temperature changes, and crystal formation. They also examine the effects of pollution and litter and develop some potential solutions to these problems. In addition, students develop an appreciation for the place of our planet in the heavens by exploring the solar system.

SOLAR SYSTEM SEARCH

KITS NEEDED: **Kit 1, 2, 3** GRADE LEVEL: **3–6**

SUGGESTED TIME: Two or three 50-minute periods

Introduction

Our solar system is composed of galaxies, stars, and planets. Our life on the planet Earth is affected to a certain degree by our planet's relationship to other objects in space. In this activity students build a model of the solar system to gather data and develop concepts about the relation of the planets.

Organization and Materials

The class should be divided into groups of four to five students each.

Per Group: Clay, ruler, planet and position chart, flashlight, construction paper, scissors, candles, thermometer.

Hint: Prior to the activity have a group of students build a model of the sun (five feet in diameter) out of construction paper and hang it near the center of the room. A discussion of scale and the scale chart may be helpful prior to this activity.

Procedure

1. Instruct students to form the clay into the planets, using the following diameters:

Mercury	⅛″
Venus	5/16″
Earth	5/16″
Mars	3/16″
Jupiter	3 ⅜″
Saturn	2 ¾″
Uranus	1 ⅛″
Neptune	1 ⅛″
Pluto	⅛″

Have groups cut rings from construction paper to form the rings around Saturn.
(MEASURING, COMMUNICATING)

2. As the groups complete their models, have the students label and arrange the planets on desks facing the sun in accordance with the position chart. (*Note:* The relative distances of the planets from the sun has been purposely eliminated. In fact, in using the scale indicated, the model of the planet Pluto would have to be placed 970 feet away from the model of the sun. Since the distance between planets is difficult to simulate, you may wish to have students consult a solar system map and then place their planets at distances they feel to be appropriate.)
(MEASURING, OBSERVING, COMMUNICATING)

3. Engage students in some of the following sample questions and activities. (Select, modify, and develop your own questions based on the ability and ages of your students. Encourage students to use their models to explain and support responses.)

"How many planets are there?" (Nine.)
(OBSERVING)

"Which planet is the largest?" (Jupiter.) "The smallest?" (Pluto; although Mercury is very small too.) "The same size as Earth?" (Venus.)
(OBSERVING, CLASSIFYING)

"How many planets are closer to the sun than Earth?" (Two.) *(OBSERVING)*

"Which planet is the closest to the sun?" (Mercury.) *(OBSERVING)*

"Which planet is the farthest from the sun?" (Pluto.) *(OBSERVING)*

"Which planet would be the hottest?" (Mercury.) "Why?" "Can you provide an answer from your everyday life to back up your answer?" (The closer one's hand is held to a heat source—a candle or lightbulb—the greater the temperature felt.) *(INFERRING, PREDICTING)*

"Which planet would be the coldest?" (Pluto.) "Why?" (It's the farthest from the sun.) "Can you provide an example from your everyday life to back up your answer?" *(INFERRING, PREDICTING)*

"What does the Earth receive from the sun?" (Heat and light.) *(INFERRING)*

"How could you show which planet would be the hottest?" "The coldest?" *(INFERRING)*

"Can you demonstrate what causes day and night?" *(INFERRING)*

"Which planet would make the farthest trip around the sun?" (Pluto.) "The shortest?" (Mercury.) "Demonstrate with your model." *(INFERRING, PREDICTING)*

Conclusion

Our solar system is made up of nine planets of varying sizes. Their proximity to the sun affects the amount of heat and light they receive. Earth is located just the right distance from the sun to support life (as we know it). Day and night are caused by the rotation of the Earth. The distance from the sun determines the length of time it takes a planet to complete an orbit.

Follow-up Activities

1. Have students make up their own questions based on their models.

2. Have students compare the sizes of the planets to determine how many times larger some are than others. They can use a ruler to help determine comparative sizes.

SKY WATCH

KITS NEEDED: **Kit 1, 3**   GRADE LEVEL: **4–6**

SUGGESTED TIME: Two 50-minute periods, with periodic observations

Introduction

The night sky offers a wide variety of interesting sights for scientific study. Stars seem to change their position, shadows are cast upon the surface of the moon, and the Earth continues to move through the heavens. These factors set the stage for the study of stars.

Organization and Materials

This activity should be done by each student individually.

Per Student: Thread, metal washer, oaktag paper, pencil, marker, clear acetate, drawing paper, tape, protractor, scissors. (*Note:* An overhead projector will be needed for class use.)

Procedure

1. Have students construct a "moon tracker" as follows: Draw a six-inch circle on oaktag and cut it out, then cut the circle in half. Mark the curved part in equal increments of 10, beginning at 10 and ending with 180. Tie the washer to the thread and tape the thread to the middle of the straight edge of the half-circle.

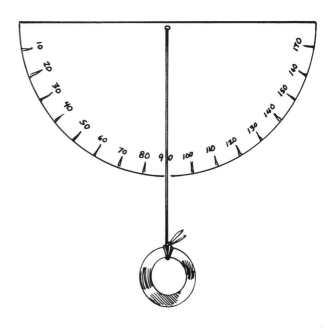

2. Tell students how to use the moon tracker by positioning the straight edge between one's eye and the top of the moon and reading the number under the thread. Direct students to take readings of the moon at the same time each night (weather permitting) for one month.

"How does the position (height) of the moon change as the month progresses?" *(OBSERVING)*

3. Have students draw a picture of the moon each night, noting the changes taking place as the month progresses.

"What happens to the shape of the moon as the month progresses?" (Refer to the Conclusion.) *(OBSERVING)*

4. Direct students to tape a piece of acetate to the inside of a house window. Have them use a marker to indicate the positions of notable groups of stars.

5. Using the overhead projector and the acetate sheets, observe the placement of the plotted stars. Have students attempt to name as many constellations as possible.

"Would these groups of stars always be at the same location throughout the year?" "Why?" (Refer to the Conclusion.) *(INFERRING)*

Conclusion

As the moon revolves around the Earth, its shape changes according to the shadow placed on it by the Earth. Stars also change their position relative to the Earth as the Earth orbits the sun.

Follow-up Activities

1. Have students locate several constellations. Direct them to draw the primary stars associated with each constellation and sketch the objects identified with each constellation. Resource books may need to be checked.

2. Have students construct a working model of a planetarium, focusing on the moon's phases and several constellations. (Punch holes, for the moon and stars, in one end of a shoebox; make a larger peephole in the other end. Shine a flashlight at the "stars" end and look through the peephole.)

CLOUDS ABOVE

KITS NEEDED: **Kit 2, 3**   GRADE LEVEL: **4—5**

SUGGESTED TIME: Three 50-minute periods, separated by several hours each

Introduction

As water evaporates from streams, ponds, oceans, and soil it rises into the upper atmosphere. Upon reaching the cooler air currents, the water vapor gathering onto small dustlike particles, thus forming clouds. Each cloud is capable of releasing its moisture onto the Earth again, setting the stage for the process to repeat itself.

Organization and Materials

This activity is best suited for groups of three to four students.

Per Group: Three large jars, two small jars, water, soil, ice, one cut plant (flower, apple, celery, etc.).

Procedure

1. Have students fill one small jar with moist soil and the other with water.

2. Direct students to cover each small jar with a large jar and to cover the plant with a large jar.

"What do you think will happen to the materials inside the jars or even to the jars themselves?" *(PREDICTING)*

3. Have students lay several ice cubes on top of the large jars. Allow the jars to stand for several hours and observe the results.

"What changes have taken place inside the jars?"

"Where did the water on the inside of the large jars come from?"

(OBSERVING, INFERRING, EXPERIMENTING)

4. Students should remove the ice and dry the inside of the large jars completely. Have them repeat the procedure by placing the jars on a shelf overnight (do not include ice in the procedure this time).

"What do you think will happen to the inside of the containers this time?"

"By not using ice, will the results be different?" *(PREDICTING)*

5. Have students examine the jars the following day, recording all similarities and differences between the trial using ice and the trial without ice.

"How can you explain the results observed in both trials?" *(COMMUNICATING)*

Conclusion

Evaporation is the physical change that takes place as water is transformed from a liquid into a gas. This gas, upon striking the cool outer jar, condensed, reversing the process and forming a liquid. This is analogous to the process that occurs during cloud formation.

Follow-up Activities

1. Using the concepts of evaporation and condensation, have students construct a diagram of the water cycle.

2. Direct pupils to complete a research project classifying clouds according to their types and functions.

EARTH **4** SCIENCE

THE SHADOW KNOWS

KITS NEEDED: **Kit 1, 2, 3**   GRADE LEVEL: **4—6**

SUGGESTED TIME: Two 50-minute periods, with periodic observations

Introduction

In the northern hemisphere the sun is always to the south of us at high noon. This position produces a shadow on the northern side of an object. By examining shadows produced by the sun, students can learn much about the direction and movement of this star.

Organization and Materials

This activity is best suited for groups of three to four students.

Per Group: Playground ball, ruler, yardstick, golf tee, flashlight, large sheet of construction paper (light colored).

Procedure

1. Direct students to stand a golf tee on end on a sheet of large construction paper.

2. Have students hold a flashlight so that it shines at different angles on the golf tee, forming various shadows on the paper.

"What happens to the shadow as the flashlight is moved to a position over the top of the tee?" (It becomes smaller.) *(OBSERVING)*

3. Have students measure the shadows at their longest and shortest lengths.

"What can you infer about the relation of the position of the light to the length of the shadow?" (Refer to the Conclusion.) *(INFERRING)*

4. Direct students to take a ruler, a yardstick, and a ball outside during the morning and place the objects on the ground (stand the ruler and yardstick on end). Have pupils record the length of the shadow formed by each object as well as the time of day each shadow was measured. Also have them measure the length of the shadow from another student and from a nearby tree.

"Do the tallest objects make the longest shadows?" "Why?"   *(OBSERVING, INFERRING)*

5. Repeat Step 4 at noon and again several hours later. Have students compare these results with their morning measurements.

"How does the length of the shadow change as the day progresses?" (Refer to the Conclusion.) *(OBSERVING)*

6. Instruct groups to construct graphs showing the lengths of the shadows observed at various times.

7. Repeat steps 4 through 6 during the remaining seasons of the year. Compare the results to those previously gathered.

"What happens to the shadows during the other seasons?" "Why?"
(OBSERVING, INFERRING)

Conclusion

Shadows are longest when the sun is at the horizon and shortest when the sun is overhead. The length of shadows is also determined by the season of the year. The relative position of the Earth to the sun affects the length of an object's shadow throughout the year.

Follow-up Activities

1. Have students draw the shapes created by the shadows of various three-dimensional objects.

2. Have students calculate the height of nearby structures by using the following formula:

$$\frac{\text{Height } (x)}{\text{Object's shadow}} = \frac{\text{Ruler}}{\text{Ruler's shadow}}$$

Example for finding the height of a tree whose shadow is fifty inches long when a ruler's shadow is three inches long:

$$\frac{x}{50} = \frac{12}{3}$$
$$3x = 600$$
$$x = 200$$

COOL IT!

KITS NEEDED: **Kit 1, 2**	GRADE LEVEL: **4–6**

SUGGESTED TIME: One 50-minute period

Introduction
Anyone getting out of a swimming pool or a bathtub is familiar with the sudden cooling off that takes place as soon as air hits the skin. This sudden change in temperature is due to the relationship that exists between air, water, and heat. These three elements, as factors in evaporation, are responsible for many aspects of our weather.

Organization and Materials
There should be two to four students per group for this activity.

Per Group: One ball of cotton, two thermometers, one piece of cardboard, water.

Procedure
1. Have each student place several drops of water on the back of his or her hand and spread it around.

"What does it feel like?"

(OBSERVING, INFERRING)

2. Have each student fan his or her hand with the piece of cardboard.

"Describe the change you feel and tell what you think is responsible for that change."

"Can you discover another way to cause this feeling?"

(EXPERIMENTING, OBSERVING, COMMUNICATING)

3. Direct pupils to wet the cotton ball and wrap it around the bulb of one of the thermometers. Record the temperature of both thermometers.

(MEASURING)

4. Have students fan the cotton-wrapped thermometer for one to two minutes.

(EXPERIMENTING)

5. Ask students to record the temperature of the cotton-wrapped thermometer after the fanning.

(MEASURING)

6. Have students fan the thermometer without the cotton and record its temperature.

(EXPERIMENTING, MEASURING)

"Is it important to fan both thermometers the same way?" "Why?" (Different methods of fanning cause variations in the results.)

(INFERRING)

7. Pupils can complete the activity by wrapping dry cotton around a thermometer and recording the temperature both before and after fanning. Also, have them put the bulb of one thermometer in water and record the results.

"Can you observe any differences in the temperature if the bulb is deep in the water rather than near the surface?"

(EXPERIMENTING, MEASURING, OBSERVING)

Conclusion
The process of cooling that took place is a result of evaporation. The heat from both the back of the hand and the mercury inside the thermometer was transferred to the air. The cooling of the mercury caused it to contract, thus lowering the temperature. The rate of evaporation, or cooling, was determined by the rate of fanning.

Follow-up Activities
1. Using the same setup, have students experiment with various fabrics and liquids to determine whether either the rate or the time of evaporation can be altered significantly or stabilized.
2. Complete this experiment on a dry day and on a wet day (or in a shower stall). Let students determine whether the surrounding environment (relative humidity) affects the rate of evaporation.

LEAKY SOIL

KITS NEEDED: **Kit 1, 2, 3**   GRADE LEVEL: **4—6**

SUGGESTED TIME: One 50-minute period

Introduction

Many types of materials cover the surface of the Earth. Each of these materials has characteristics and qualities that can be both advantageous and disadvantageous to the animals and plants that inhabit the surroundings. This project examines the ability of water to pass through various types of soil—an important consideration for farmers and home gardeners.

Organization and Materials

This project is best suited for groups of two to three students.

Per Group: Various soil samples to be studied (peat moss, potting soil, sand, pebbles, clay soil, and so on)—one-half metric cup of each, paper cups, plastic cups, pencils, two popsicle sticks per cup, one paper towel, water, a clock or watch with a second hand.

Procedure

1. Have students examine each sample and list its characteristics.
(OBSERVING, COMMUNICATING)
2. Direct pupils to use a pencil to poke ten or twelve holes in the bottom of each paper cup.
3. Have students place a piece of paper towel in the bottom of each paper cup to prevent the granules of each sample from falling out.
4. Ask students to fill each of the cups exactly half-full with the various samples and label each container with the name of its contents.
5. Instruct students to place two popsicle sticks across the tops of the plastic cups to form a bridge and to set the paper cups on top of the sticks (this allows water to flow into the plastic cups).
6. Tell students to fill each paper cup (one by one) with water and time how long it takes before water begins to seep through into the plastic cups. Have them record the results.
(MEASURING, COMMUNICATING)
7. Discuss the findings. (Refer to the Conclusion.)

"Which sample permitted water to seep through first?"

"Which sample was the slowest in showing signs of water seeping through?"
"Did each sample allow the same amount of water to seep through?"
"Can you explain why?"
"Where is the remainder of the water?"
(COMMUNICATING, CLASSIFYING, MEASURING, INFERRING)

"What advantages or disadvantages would each of the samples have if it covered the Earth in a particular area?"
"How would the plants and animals have to adapt to each area?"
(INFERRING, COMMUNICATING)

Conclusion

Results will depend on the samples used. Some samples (peat moss, potting soil) allow water to pass through very quickly compared to others, such as sand. However, those same samples retain more water than sand does.

Follow-up Activities

1. Have students measure the amount of water retained by each sample (amount poured in minus the amount collected in the plastic cup).
2. Ask students to predict which samples would be most conducive to the growth of various kinds of plant life (such as sand for cactus, peat moss for ferns). Provide opportunities for pupils to grow various varieties of plants in different soil samples and record their results.

DIRT CHEAP

KITS NEEDED: **Kit 1, 2, 3**   GRADE LEVEL: **4—5**

SUGGESTED TIME: One 50-minute period

Introduction
Depending on the geographical location, the surrounding environment, climatic conditions, and other factors, soil can be composed of many different materials. Soil composition in turn affects the plant life—and subsequently the animal life—that inhabits the particular area.

Organization and Materials
Individuals or pairs of students can complete this activity.

Per Group: Newspaper to cover desk, a plastic bag of soil, a piece of white construction paper (twelve inches by seventeen inches), one large toothpick, a magnifying glass, and a sheet of paper to record data.

Note: Prior to beginning this activity, direct students to cover their desks with newspaper. Upon completion of the activity, have students work in pairs to carefully fold the white paper and funnel the soil back into the bags.

Procedure
1. Begin the activity with a brief discussion of what covers the Earth.

"What is the composition of the Earth?" (Rock, soil, sand, water, and so on.)

"What covers the Earth?" (Soil, plants, and so on.) *(COMMUNICATING, OBSERVING)*

2. "Today we are going to look at one of the materials that cover our Earth—soil. Does anyone know what soil is?" (Accept answers that students can support with evidence.) *(COMMUNICATING, INFERRING)*

3. Distribute the soil samples, white construction paper, toothpicks, and magnifying glasses.

4. Instruct the students to empty the bag of soil onto the white paper. Students should be encouraged to keep the soil on the white paper throughout the activity. After the bags have been emptied, have the students observe their samples, instructing them to (a) separate into groups the various kinds of substances they find (using the toothpick), and (b) make a list of the various substances discovered. *(OBSERVING, CLASSIFYING, COMMUNICATING)*

5. After five to ten minutes, discuss the findings with the class.

"What types of substances did you find in the soil?" (Roots, leaves, small stones, possibly dead insects, and so on.)

"Where do we usually find these kinds of substances?" (Growing or living near or in the soil.)

"How do you think these substances got into the soil?"

"What did you find the most?"

"Describe (or list) the characteristics of each substance."

"Where does soil originate?" (Refer to the Conclusion.) *(OBSERVING, CLASSIFYING, COMMUNICATING, INFERRING, PREDICTING)*

Conclusion
Soil is composed of bits of wood, leaves, roots, insects, plants, and small stones. As the organic substances die and decay, they turn into soil.

Follow-up Activities
1. Ask students whether there is anything in the soil that they were unable to see with their eyes or the magnifying lens. If students say water or air, ask them how they can prove this. (To check for water, soil can be heated to detect steam. To check for air, water can be added to a small soil sample and observed for the appearance of bubbles.)

2. Have students collect and examine soil from various outdoor areas (woods, stream bank, open field) and discuss and chart their findings.

SOIL SHAKE

KITS NEEDED: **Kit 2, 3**   **GRADE LEVEL:** **5–6**

SUGGESTED TIME: One 50-minute period

Introduction

As we dig in our gardens or yards we often notice that the composition of the soil changes the deeper we dig. The many different kinds of materials that make up soil form layers, depending on their composition or relative weights. In this project various soil samples are mixed with water to demonstrate how sediment layers are formed.

Organization and Materials

Divide the class into groups of three to four each.

Per Group: Soil samples (approximately one-half metric cup each of humus, garden soil, peat moss, clay, and so on), a jar and lid for each sample, water, magnifying glass.

Procedure

1. Have the students place approximately six centimeters of each soil sample in clean jars and label each jar.   *(COMMUNICATING)*

2. Instruct the students to examine the soil sample in Jar 1 and list its characteristics. *(OBSERVING, COMMUNICATING)*

3. Have students fill the rest of the jar with water and put the lid on.

4. "Shake the jar for thirty seconds and observe and describe the results."

"Has the water changed?"

"Describe the soil at the bottom?" (Bigger particles.)   *(OBSERVING, COMMUNICATING)*

5. Have the students observe the soil and water in the jar for one or two minutes and list their observations.   *(OBSERVING, COMMUNICATING)*

6. Have students repeat steps 2 through 5 for each sample.   *(OBSERVING, COMMUNICATING)*

7. Have students compare the findings for the various samples.

"How does the water of one sample compare to that of another?"

"Are the layers of sediment the same or different between samples?"

"How do the layers differ between individual samples?"

Conclusion

Soil is composed of numerous particles, ranging from minute sandlike pieces to somewhat larger pieces of gravel or wood. When soil is mixed with water and allowed to settle, layers are formed. The bottom layer contains the largest and heaviest particles, with successively higher layers containing smaller and smaller particles. The lightest particles float on the surface of the water.

Follow-up Activities

1. Have students pour the samples into paper cups and place them in the sun. Allow the water to evaporate (it can be removed with an eyedropper for faster results). When soil samples dry, have students peel off the paper cups and examine the sediments formed.

2. Have students measure and record the daily evaporation of the water from each sample.

"Does the composition of the soil affect the evaporation rate of the water?"

"What soil characteristics foster slower evaporation rates?"

"Would this information be helpful to know?" "Why?"

SPLISH SPLASH

| KITS NEEDED: | **Kit 2, 3** | GRADE LEVEL: | **4—5** |

| SUGGESTED TIME: | One 50-minute period |

Introduction

Erosion is responsible for the loss of a great deal of land and coastal property. Such loss can be reduced, however, by use of careful planning and corrective measures.

Organization and Materials

This activity is best completed in groups of six to seven students. Each group should use a different soil medium.

Per Group: One twelve-by-eighteen container (cake dish), a soil sample, modeling clay, a marble, a golfball, a baseball, rulers.

Procedure

1. Tell students to place soil at one end of the container, being certain that the soil is at least as high as the container's side.

2. Have pupils fill the remainder of the container with water (the water level should be no more than halfway up the medium).

3. Direct students to drop each of the following into the water several times and observe the medium's reaction to the waves as they strike it: marble, golfball, baseball.

"What conclusion can be drawn about the larger objects dropped into the water?" (The larger the object, the larger the wave.)
(OBSERVING, INFERRING)

4. Have students alter the frequency of the object dropping (every four seconds, then every three seconds, and so on). Observe and record the changes that take place.

"What happens to both the water and the medium as the frequency of the dropping is increased?" *(OBSERVING)*

5. "Which of the mediums seems to erode the quickest?" "The least?" "Why?"
(EXPERIMENTING, OBSERVING, INFERRING)

6. Discuss with students how constant wave action affects the shoreline of an ocean or lake.

"How would waves affect the erosion of a shoreline?" (They would increase the rate of shoreline erosion.)

"What measures could be used to retard this erosion?" (Shoreline plantings or rocks placed along the shore.) *(INFERRING, COMMUNICATING)*

7. Have students use rulers or clay to construct breakwaters or jettys in their containers to slow down or prevent wave damage. Pictures of harbors may be shown to illustrate this principle.

"Why are these jettys important?" (They stop the waves and thereby reduce the amount of erosion.)

"Should humans interfere with the natural course of nature?" *(INFERRING)*

Conclusion

The more compact the soil, the less likely it is to be influenced by the forces responsible for erosion. Likewise, when soil is protected by other barriers its rate of erosion can be greatly reduced or even eliminated.

Follow-up Activities

1. Have students repeat this activity altering the direction and force of the waves by holding a ruler on the surface of the water.

2. Have students plant grass seed on the soil and compare the results of wave action on both planted and unplanted surfaces.

TAKE A DIP

KITS
NEEDED: **Kit 2, 3**   GRADE
LEVEL: **4—5**

SUGGESTED
TIME: One 50-minute period

Introduction
Water has varying effects on different substances. It may be extremely damaging or have no effect at all. The consistency of the object, the water temperature, movement or stillness of the water, and content of the water are factors that must be considered. In this activity students will observe the effects water has on objects. Various objects are observed both before and after being placed in water.

Organization and Materials
Divide class into groups of two to four each.

Per Group: Items to be tested (three samples of each, with one serving as a control): sugar cubes, salt, crackers, soil, chalk, iced tea mix, buttons, paper towels, dried soup, flour, and so on; a magnifying glass, a jar and plastic cup for each of the tested samples, warm and cold water.

Procedure
1. "What happens to various objects when placed in water?" (They become soft, fall apart, get wet, and so on.)
(INFERRING, COMMUNICATING)
2. Have the students observe and list the characteristics of each of the samples to be tested. Have them use magnifying glasses to double-check their observations, and discuss the findings.
(OBSERVING, COMMUNICATING)
3. Have the students place the items to be tested in jars of cold water and observe the results. Have them list the changes observed and record the time needed for items to change.
(OBSERVING, COMMUNICATING, MEASURING)

4. Discuss the results. Have the students describe each substance and the changes observed after one to two minutes.   *(COMMUNICATING)*
5. "Is there anything that can be done to the water that may change the results for a particular item?" Have students predict results for each change (stirring the water, warming the water, adding salt, and so on).   *(PREDICTING)*
6. Have the students test each object in warm water and discuss the results.
(OBSERVING, MEASURING, COMMUNICATING)
7. Have students compare results for warm water versus those obtained in cold water.
   "Did the objects change faster or more slowly?"
(CLASSIFYING, COMMUNICATING)
8. Ask students to brainstorm a list of items that are changed as a result of being immersed in water and a list of those that do not change. Have students bring in various items for testing. Provide opportunities for students to chart their results.

Conclusion
Water may or may not have an effect on items placed in it. Sometimes both the water and the item change noticeably, sometimes only the item changes, and sometimes neither changes. Warm water speeds up changes, whereas cold water tends to slow down any changes.

Follow-up Activities
1. Have students test objects in salt water, vinegar, and other liquids.
2. Have students test the long-term effects of emersing various items in water.
3. "Is there a way to slow down the changes that occur?"

PASS THE SALT

KITS NEEDED: **Kit 2, 3**   GRADE LEVEL: **4—6**

SUGGESTED TIME: One 50-minute period

Introduction

The Earth is covered by various types of water. These types have many differences. Salt water is less transparent, has a stronger smell, is denser, and impedes the dissolving rate of many materials in comparison to fresh water. In this project some of the characteristics of salt water and fresh water are explored. Students test the buoyancy and dissolving rates of various objects when placed in both kinds of water.

Organization and Materials

This activity is designed for groups of three to four students.

Per Group: Two tall glasses or jars, water, two teaspoons of salt, a stirrer, a magnifying glass, two sugar cubes, two pieces of hard candy, other objects to be tested (such as noodles, small pieces of carrot, rice).

Procedure

1. Have groups fill two tall glasses with ten to twenty centimeters of water. They should place two spoonfuls of salt in one of the glasses and stir until dissolved.   *(MEASURING)*

2. Have the students observe, list, and discuss the characteristics of the contents of both glasses. (For example: Salt Water—cloudy, appears thicker, smells; Plain Water—clear, contains tiny bubbles.)

(OBSERVING, COMMUNICATING, CLASSIFYING)

3. Have students place a pair of objects to be tested (such as noodles, rice) in the two glasses simultaneously and record observations (a watch or clock with a second hand may be used to record sinking, floating, or dissolving rates). Have students remove the objects from both glasses before testing another pair.

"Did the (object tested) sink or float?"

"Did the two objects sink at the same speed?"

"Did the objects react differently in the two liquids?"

"Why do you think the objects behaved the way they did?"

(OBSERVING, MEASURING, COMMUNICATING, PREDICTING)

4. "Now place a sugar cube in each glass and observe what happens."

"In which glass did the sugar dissolve the fastest?"

"Did they dissolve differently?"

5. "Place a small piece of hard candy in each glass and compare dissolving rates again."

"Describe what happened."

(OBSERVING, COMMUNICATING)

Conclusion

Certain materials are more buoyant in salt water than plain water, because of the higher density of salt water. The density of salt water also impedes the dissolving rate of many materials.

Follow-up Activities

1. Have students time the dissolving rates of various objects.

2. Have pupils determine the buoyancy of various liquids. This can be done by floating a jar lid on the surface of each liquid and calculating the amount of weight needed to sink the lid by placing pennies (one by one) on the lid.

WARMING UP

KITS NEEDED: **Kit 2, 3**   GRADE LEVEL: **4—6**

SUGGESTED TIME: One 50-minute period

Introduction

Sand, soil, air, and water are some of the substances that make up the surface of our Earth. However, they are affected differently by the heat from the sun.

Organization and Materials

This activity is intended for groups of two to four students and should be done on a sunny day.

Per Group: One to four thermometers, magnifying glasses, various samples three-fourths cup each of tap water, soil, and sand.

Procedure

1. Hand out materials. "Carefully examine all the samples and list their characteristics."
(OBSERVING, COMMUNICATING)

2. Discuss the students' observations.
   "Describe each of the samples."
   "How do the samples differ? How are they alike?"
   "Which samples do you think will warm up most when placed in a sunny area?"
(COMMUNICATING, CLASSIFYING, INFERRING)

3. Have the students measure and record (a) the air temperature, (b) the temperature of a cup of water, (c) the soil temperature (by carefully inserting the thermometer into the soil), and (d) the sand temperature.
(MEASURING, COMMUNICATING)

4. Discuss and compare readings.
   "Were all readings the same?" (No.)
   "Look at each sample again and refer to your earlier observations. Can you explain the different temperatures recorded?" (Accept all hypotheses.)   *(COMMUNICATING, INFERRING)*

5. Direct students to place each sample in the sunlight for twenty to twenty-five minutes. While waiting, students can predict and record what they think will occur, continue the discussion from Step 4, or construct graphs of temperature readings from Step 3.
(PREDICTING, COMMUNICATING, MEASURING)

6. After twenty to twenty-five minutes, have the students measure and record the temperature of each sample.   *(MEASURING, COMMUNICATING)*

7. Compare and discuss readings.
   "What happened to the readings?"
   "Did all of the readings increase?"
   "Did the readings increase by the same amount?"
   "Can you offer possible explanations based on your previous observations?" (Refer to the Conclusion.)
(CLASSIFYING, COMMUNICATING, MEASURING, INFERRING)

Conclusion

The soil sample should register the greatest gain in temperature, while the sand, water, and air samples follow in order. The dark color of the soil makes it absorb more heat than the other substances, hence increasing the temperature faster.

Follow-up Activities

1. Have students measure and record heat loss when samples are placed in ice or in cold water.

2. Students can measure temperature gain for various containers (dark, tin foiled), with and without lids.

3. Have students initiate long-term studies on a variety of samples (leaves, grass, polluted pond water, lemonade, clay, humus, wood chips, and so on) and chart the variations in temperature.

DON'T BREATHE!

KITS
NEEDED: **Kit 1, 2**   GRADE
LEVEL: **4—6**

SUGGESTED
TIME: Two 50-minute periods

Introduction

Many kinds of particulate matter pollute our air. Both natural and human-made situations are responsible for these pollutants. By closely examining our environment we can locate some of the causes of this pollution and can better control it.

Organization and Materials

This activity is best suited for groups of three to four students.

Per Group: Clear cellophane, petroleum jelly, index cards, drawing paper, a magnifying glass, a microscope, tape.

Procedure

1. Direct students to tape a two-inch by two-inch piece of clear cellophane on the back of an index card (each group should prepare five of these cards).

2. Have pupils rub a thin film of petroleum jelly onto the cellophane and number each card.

3. Direct students to prepare an outline map of the inside of your school building.

4. Have students mount the cards throughout the school, recording the location of each card on the map. (*Hint:* Place the cards in locations where activities differ. Also, mount them at different heights.)

"Why is it beneficial to hang the cards at different heights in different areas of the school?" (Pollution rates may vary according to height.)
(INFERRING)

5. After one week have students collect the cards.

6. Have students examine the cards closely using either a magnifying glass or a microscope. Have students classify the cards according to degrees of pollutants found on each.

"Which area in the school seems to have the most air pollution?"

"How can this be explained?"
(OBSERVING, INFERRING)

7. Graph the results and discuss ideas for improving the air in your building.   *(MEASURING)*

Conclusion

Air pollution levels vary depending on the type of activity taking place in a specific area. This pollution becomes part of the air we breathe. The cumulative effects of pollutants may eventually affect our health or level of activity.

Follow-up Activities

1. Expand the activity by having students examine the amount of air pollution throughout your community. Pollution cards can be placed in several stores or municipal buildings as well as various outdoor locations.

2. Have students present a plan to the proper authorities suggesting ways to decrease the amount of air pollution in the school or community.

SLOW DOWN!

KITS NEEDED: **Kit 1, 2, 3**   GRADE LEVEL: **4—6**

SUGGESTED TIME: One 50-minute period

Introduction

Seeing a person slowly and safely falling to earth beneath a parachute is quite intriguing. However, not just any piece of cloth will provide a safe descent. The proper type and amount of chute and length of rope or string determine the efficient operation of the device. Students construct a parachute that fails to work properly. In turn, they are challenged to use problem-solving skills to devise a better chute and develop an explanation as to why it operates more efficiently.

Organization and Materials

Divide class into groups of two to three each.

Demonstration Materials: Pencil, ball, egg.

Per Group: One paper cup, cellophane tape, approximately thirty centimeters of string, five to ten small washers, large pan.

Additional Chute Materials: Paper napkin, paper towel, plastic sandwich bag, newspaper sheet.

Procedure

1. Demonstrate the principle of gravity. "What happens if I let go of this pencil, this ball, or this egg?" (Drop the egg over a large pan.)
(OBSERVING, COMMUNICATING)

2. "Do you know what causes the objects to fall to the ground?" (Accept answers that students are able to conceptualize based on age and ability—weight, size, gravity, and so on.)
(INFERRING, COMMUNICATING)

3. "Suppose you were to fall out of an airplane. What would happen?"
(INFERRING, COMMUNICATING)

4. "Is there any way you could slow down your fall?"   *(INFERRING, COMMUNICATING)*

"Let's investigate and construct parachutes."

5. Give each group a paper cup, string, tape, and a small washer. Have the students construct a parachute by taping or tying strings at equal intervals around the rim of the cup and tying the washer to the end of the strings.

6. Instruct the students to stand on a chair and drop the cup parachute.

"Did it work?"

"What happened?"

(OBSERVING, COMMUNICATING)

7. "How could we improve our parachute?" (Students may suggest longer or shorter strings, less weight, and so on.)

Allow students to test their hypotheses (none of the suggested changes will radically improve the chute since the problem is the weight of the cup itself).   *(COMMUNICATING, INFERRING)*

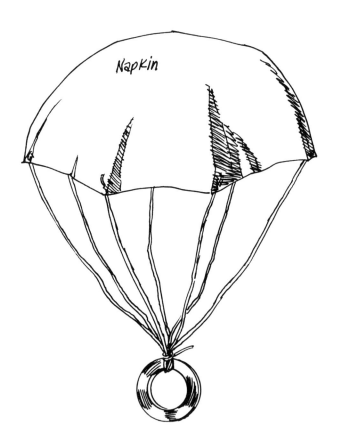

Napkin

8. Permit students to use the additional chute materials or other substitutions to develop the best possible parachute.

"Which material worked best? Can you explain why?"

"Did the newspaper sheet work as well as the paper napkin?" (No.)

"What do you think the problem may have been with the newspaper?" (Too large or too heavy.)

"What slows the parachute down?" or "What is under the paper as it falls?" (Air.)

(OBSERVING, EXPERIMENTING, COMMUNICATING, INFERRING)

Conclusion

Larger parachutes have more air beneath them and consequently fall more slowly. However, a point is reached at which a chute becomes too large or heavy for the suspended weight and does not function properly.

Follow-up Activities

1. Have the students attach fragile items (such as raw eggs) to various chutes to determine the most efficient relationship between weight and chute size. More advanced students may wish to construct special charts that plot weight versus chute size versus string length to determine optimum characteristics.

2. Have students compare equal-sized chutes of various materials (cloth, paper, plastic, and so on).

Dear Parents,

Helping your child grow in science will be an important part of our studies this year. Your child will be able to examine the wide world of science through a variety of exciting and interesting science projects.

Many of our projects will require the use of materials commonly found in the home. Could you please assist us by offering to donate some of the items on the attached list? Your child has checked those that he or she feels you may be able to contribute. Whatever else you can donate will certainly be appreciated. Please feel free to contact me if you have any questions or concerns. Thank you in advance.

Sincerely,

- ☐ food coloring
- ☐ clay
- ☐ waxed paper
- ☐ crayons
- ☐ scissors
- ☐ measuring cup
- ☐ knives
- ☐ paper cups
- ☐ stopwatch
- ☐ string
- ☐ paper towels
- ☐ seeds
- ☐ candles
- ☐ sugar
- ☐ cardboard
- ☐ cotton balls
- ☐ salt
- ☐ wool
- ☐ bobby pins
- ☐ pepper
- ☐ wire

- ☐ plastic wrap—one roll
- ☐ coat hangers
- ☐ marbles
- ☐ birdseed
- ☐ paint
- ☐ aluminum foil
- ☐ sponges
- ☐ masking tape
- ☐ colored cellophane
- ☐ spoons
- ☐ jars
- ☐ magnifying glass
- ☐ thermometer
- ☐ newspaper
- ☐ toothpicks
- ☐ copper wire
- ☐ magnets
- ☐ baking soda
- ☐ plastic bags
- ☐ coffee cans
- ☐ cigar box

- ☐ corks
- ☐ petroleum jelly
- ☐ stockings
- ☐ styrofoam cups
- ☐ baby food jars
- ☐ teaspoons
- ☐ jar lids
- ☐ baseball
- ☐ liquid bleach
- ☐ paper bags
- ☐ golf tees
- ☐ golf balls
- ☐ silicon glue
- ☐ straws
- ☐ metal washers
- ☐ shoe boxes
- ☐ pill or film containers
- ☐ plastic gallon milk cartons
- ☐ yogurt containers with lids
- ☐ shallow cake dish
- ☐ cereal

RECORDING CHARTS

One of the most important aspects of a process approach to science is the recording of data. The recorded information helps students understand relationships, patterns, and the long-term results of their projects. Recording data also helps students value their investigations as well as their accumulation of new knowledge.

The charts that follow are generic; that is, they have been designed to be used for a variety of projects and activities. You are encouraged to work with your students in selecting not only an appropriate chart for any project but also the way in which the resultant data will be recorded.

These charts can also be used as measuring devices for selected activities. When placed behind a plant or under a worm they are appropriate for recording growth or movement. Students may want to note their measurements in terms of standard or metric units or by "squares."

You may want to duplicate these charts and laminate them. This option permits students to use the charts over and over again throughout the year. Another possibility would be to transfer the charts to overhead transparencies in order to use them for whole-class viewing. However you plan to use the charts, they can and should be a valuable part of each student's investigations into the world of science.
